essays on the
environment
of wales

green
agenda

essays on the
environment
of wales

green
agenda

ed. robert minhinnick

seren

seren is the imprint of
Poetry Wales Press Ltd
Wyndham Street, Bridgend
Mid Glamorgan, Wales

Selection, editorial & introduction
© Robert Minhinnick, 1994

Content of essays © John Barnie, Neil Caldwell,
Rory Francis, Alwyn Jones, Nic Lampkin,
Peter Midmore, Margaret Minhinnick,
Alan Watson, Phil Williams, 1994

ISBN: 1-85411-101-9

*seren works with the financial assistance
of the Arts Council of Wales*

cover illustration: detail from 'The Dream' by Kim Waale

*The publisher is grateful to Dŵr Cymru Welsh Water and
the Countryside Council for Wales for their generous
sponsorship of Alan Watson's research for his essay*

Printed in Palatino by Cromwell Press, Melksham
on recycled paper

Contents

...we cannot allow our proper concern to blind us to man-kind's need to change and develop. A society which does not grow is one which cannot satisfy some of our basic human needs... Economic development is just as important a concept as environmental protection, and we must find ways of achieving both together.

Introduction to *Sustainable Development: The UK Strategy, 1994*

With most environmentalists shy about asserting that each struggle was part of a larger, grander issue, each battle was fought as if isolated from the others. So careful were we not to be thought too radical that we rarely exposed the real problem: a system of logic, and a set of assumptions, that led to the problems of dams, pesticides, nukes, growth, and the rest of it. Meanwhile, industry, the media, and the government were all repeating the mantra that technology serves progress, and that progress equals more technology. And at each stage of technical development, we fell more deeply into the techno-maelstrom.

Jeremy Mander *In the Absence of the Sacred*

Save and keep me
From the wind that is blowing where it will.

James Kitchener Davies

Introduction

Like it or not, our society has created a culture in which appearance is more important than substance, and the power of the image far transcends that of truth. Taliesin, the first Welsh environmentalist, and a great myth-weaver and poet, who (possibly) flourished fourteen hundred years ago, would surely have approved of this. However, the chasm between what is perceived and what is real has now grown so great that it threatens the roots of our identity. This applies especially, and sometimes spectacularly, to what this volume describes as 'the environment of Wales'.

To accept our roles as citizens of a world of image-marketing, the sanitising of history as 'heritage', and the frenzied manufacture of news or 'information' into a product to be consumed like fast-food, is to succumb to the dogma that Wales has an image problem. The dogma would have it that socially, we remain a working-class country when elsewhere the working-class is busy reinventing itself: that militarily, we are England's little butty, as loyal as the Ghurkas: that culturally, as that acute and depressingly representative critic, A.N. Wilson, has described, we are dingy and untalented. Yet whatever the factuality behind such legendeering, Wales is far more affected by a false perception of its physical identity than by the above mythology.

Despite the commercially heroic efforts of the massed advertising agencies hired by Cardiff Bay Development Corporation to 'sell' the 'regeneration' of the capital, Wales remains seriously damaged, at least in our world of instant opinion and flash-card philosophy, by a primitive stereotyping of the environment. Thus the north consists of pristine mountain ranges and breathtaking scenery. The *canolbarth*, in the eyes of English immigrants and moss-green idealists, offers one of the last 'wilderness' areas in the

UK. The south is a region of slag, stilled pit wheels and high-tech Japanese factories employing low-skilled Welsh workers. Only one thing has been more marginalised by propaganda, lethargic thought and vested interests than the environment, and that is the concept of 'environmentalism' itself.

This is partly because the Welsh environmental movement is a very strange animal indeed. Crudely, it can be classified as three breeds. Best established are the members of the county wildlife organisations and the National Trust. These people are largely middle-aged (or older), middle-class, and basically well-to-do. Their politics are Conservative and old-style Liberal. Their interests are in protecting the countryside and its more interesting habitats and features. Corncrakes, water-meadows and long-houses are important to them. Socially, they are a fascinating sub-strata themselves, largely unchronicled by our working-class-fixated historians.

The second group consists (again, roughly) of English incomers, retreating from lost causes to the east, and bringing with them a confused idealism that has often been perplexing to the native Welsh. These are the stalwarts of the 1970s and 80s green movement, who at one period, approximately five years ago, appeared to be on the brink of a real political and lifestyle breakthrough. The failure of that change to occur has seriously eroded their morale and campaigning energy.

The third grouping comprises the researchers and academics who find employment in our universities and now with the Countryside Council for Wales. These are the scientific men and women, who, crucially, do not rely on tradition, instinct or intimations of apocalypse to impel their work. Their approach is unemotional and they deal in proof. They have much to teach us. The problem is, such is the compartmentalisation of science and the rigidity of disciplines, that there currently exists very little dialogue between the academics, let alone success in reaching the public. To everyone's cost, science is either mute or inept at communicating its messages.

As to the majority of the Welsh public, it has ignored all three of the above breeds. The issues that have obsessed the middle-class conservationists, the radical greens and the scientists, such as the 'integrity' of National Parks, the effects of acidification and the development of wind-power, have been deemed as irrelevant. This has also been the reaction of the major political parties in Wales to environmental debate. Labour and the Conservatives have gleefully abandoned green issues to the vociferous lobbyists of the pressure groups. The party apparatchiks rightly perceived that these much-quoted organisations were devoting all their time and money to matters that had no lasting popular appeal. What might have proved a political threat and an irresistible challenge to orthodoxy was exhausting itself on a round of self-imposed wild-goose chases.

The pressure groups' insistence on the importance of long-term planning has cut no political ice simply because UK politics is utterly short-termist. Evidence for this is the failure to budget seriously for the decommissioning costs of our nuclear reactors, estimated by the National Audit Office at £18 billion. That is only one of the economic swords of Damocles suspended above us, created by environmental ignorance.

Yet it cannot be claimed that the Welsh majority have no environmental interest. Concerned with employment, health and education, the urban Welsh of Deeside, Wrexham, Cardiff and the Valleys, together with the agricultural communities of the hinterland, have continually indicated that environmentalism will only succeed where it is most closely aligned with quality of life and immediacy of threat. The irony is, that after years of tub-thumping and media opportunities for worthy but largely obscure causes, pressure groups such as Friends of the Earth are now modifying their approach, and reacting to what could be described as the populist messages they have previously put to one side.

To be fair, work that provides jobs whilst benefiting the environment has long been a necessity perceived by green groups. They acknowledge that the very concept of 'work' has been corrupted, and that the rigid institutionalisation and reward-system of employment lead to social and environmental evil. The stigma and false associations of the word 'unemployed' create the impetus for this.

Yet full employment in the UK seems now unachievable. Throughout the nineties, ten per cent of the Welsh workforce has remained 'unemployed' (though not necessarily unoccupied) whilst a vast amount of important work in our communities is left undone. The success of the 'Resourcesaver' recycling and energy conservation scheme in Bristol in the mid-eighties and the later 'Community Service Anti-Waste Scheme' in Cardiff are testament to the alternatives to inactivity and introspection. At their peak they created hundreds of jobs but were largely dependent on grants from agencies such as the Manpower Services Commission. They were remarkable as much for their rarity as for what they achieved.

Thus environmentalism in Wales and elsewhere, the belated wisdom dictates, should now fully engage with employment and the concept of work; must directly link pollution with health, and life quality with lifestyle; and should be fully integrated into the educational system instead of providing frogspawn-in-a-jamjar-style interludes from 'real' teaching. At last the plethora of UK and international pressure groups that work on environmental matters are beginning to realise that a global or national campaign style is meaningless, and that different regions, classes and cultures require individual treatment. Organisations such as Greenpeace have believed for too long that the global audience consists of middle-class families who have nothing better to talk about over their organic cornflakes than Antarctic whaling or cargoes of toxic waste.

Perhaps there is no clearer example of the environment movement's failure to accept political reality than its attitude to the Welsh language. Proponents of green culture must recognise that the health of *yr hen iaith*, which is spoken by almost twenty per cent of our 2.9 million population, is an essential environmental issue. So are the startling demographic changes that have occurred here in the past twenty-five years. For instance, there are now more English-born residents of Wales than there are Welsh speakers. In many former bastions of what might crudely be called 'the Welsh way of life', these 'incomers' comprise up to forty per cent of the population. (The major irony here is that if 'Welshness' is defined by birth, then the most Welsh areas in the world are the former mining valleys of Glamorgan and Gwent. In districts such as the Rhondda, over ninety per cent of the people are native born. Of course many of these are the descendants of Irish, English and Italian 'incomers' attracted by the industrial boom.)

However, there are Friends of the Earth groups in areas like

Ceredigion and Dinefwr comprised almost entirely of English people. This type of unintentional apartheid is little short of tragic. The decision by a Green Party candidate in local elections in Arfon to issue an English-only campaign leaflet because he "did not wish to make language an issue" has already become part of folklore in the area.

Likewise the hostility of language campaigners to the green movement is melancholy proof of the narrowing, even embittering, result of one-issue lobbying. The gulf of suspicion and incomprehension between these two forces for change and empowerment has been to the detriment and credibility of both. It was probably best expressed by Dafydd Iwan in an article titled 'What I understand by conservation' in the first issue of *Planet* in 1971. He wrote:

> Just as our physical environment is being eroded, so also is our cultural environment, and of the two, the latter is of more fundamental and lasting importance. So, if we're talking of conservation, let us put first things first...
>
> ...Instead, therefore, of talking merely about conserving the countryside, let us conserve and revitalise the indigenous communities of that same countryside. This, of course, is applicable to many rural areas of Britain to some degree. But in Wales there is an even more serious aspect to it all, since these rapidly declining rural areas are also the areas of predominantly Welsh-speaking people, where the cultural heritage is at its most pure. Thus the exodus from our countryside is also sapping the life-blood of our cultural life, and the remaining communities suffer a further two-pronged attack on their Welshness — from the mass media, and from a rapidly increasing influx of English speakers as weekenders, summer-dwellers and retired people.

Leaving aside the dangerous reference to cultural purity, these twenty-five year old words are as relevant now as at the time of writing. That, in itself, is disturbing, for in the generation since they were published, the language and environment movements have remained aloof from each other. No individual with sufficient respect and authority has emerged to discuss uniting the campaigns, and there is no current dialogue. Thus Welsh tribalism maintains its souring influence and an obvious political opportunity goes begging.

This is especially galling, considering the failure of the Wales Green Party to develop a community base. This tiny group of idealists (it would say 'realists') remains a seed-bed of often attractive philosophies and paper policies. The pressure groups, worn down by the banal minutiae of issues and ceaseless reactive campaigning, have long sought from it the nourishment of ideas. This is not surprising. Pressure groups are often intellectual vacuums. The kind of debate they encourage usually concerns the nature of their own image. In terms of economics, which has overall control of the quality of the environment, they are both illiterate and innumerate. However, as far as political influence goes, Green Party importance is negligible in the UK. Considering it took fifteen per cent of the vote in the 1989 European elections, this ineffectuality is astonishing.

In Wales, however, where there was an eleven per cent backing for the greens, the situation is slightly different. The Plaid Cymru/Green Party alliance that enabled Cynog Dafis to win the Ceredigion/Pembroke North seat in the 1992 General Election, was a notable triumph. Cynog Dafis is the only elected Member of Parliament ever to campaign on a (fifty per cent) Green ticket, and looks like remaining unique for some time to come. His victory is a tribute to the practical application of political idealism by an impressive group of Dyfed activists. The irony, however, is that outside this singular constituency, the Wales Green Party remains remote from real power.

Environmentalists should accept as a fact of life the reluctance of the public to embrace radical causes. Crucially, they must also note the fate of the peace movement. CND (a shadow of its former self) and other bodies have been rendered ineffective by sudden and swift political change. Indeed, the way that official and public interest now by-passes CND is a warning to the green groups. Chernobyl and the marine pollution that seemed to threaten UK seal populations were two of the issues that helped create a conflagration of public environmental interest. Too much of that concern has hardened into a cynicism that sees dangers like caesium contamination of Gwynedd or PCBs in Gwent as inevitable as bad weather.

Thus if the period 1987-91 was the pinnacle of influence achieved by environmental campaigning, the near future might well be dominated by the aid agencies as they increasingly radicalise their messages, and also by protest networks reacting against the squalor, pollution and crime in UK cities. The integration of environmentalism into organisations such as Oxfam, Action Aid and the World Development Movement, together with housing, health and lifestyle groups, is now a challenge and a necessity. Also of importance are a variety of organisations specifically opposed to the Government's new roads programme. These range from teepee-dwellers to disaffected Tories appalled by the destruction of Twyford Down and the proposed, so-called 'M48' that could destroy the reen-cut wetlands of the Gwent Levels. The overall imperative for the leading pressure groups is therefore adapt or meet that worst of all possible fates: irrelevance.

As to Welsh language politics, its failure to address properly the exploration for oil and gas between Clwyd and south Pembrokeshire is the most recent evidence of the damning division of the modest pool of Welsh activists into linguistic and environmental camps. The possible exploitation of hydrocarbons poses massive threats and opportunities for the future health of the language well into the next century. Yet Wales' most uncompromising pressure group, *Cymdeithas yr Iaith*, has backed away from the subject.

If oil and gas exploration is not the issue to wed green activists with the Welsh Language Society, perhaps the catalyst will be water. As the atmosphere warms because of the pollution we pour into it, and the climate changes, some parts of the world will become wetter, others drier. Whilst it is impossible to predict, it seems possible that Wales will remain famous for its water wealth, whilst the south of England runs dangerously dry. Despite the initial expense, there are now discussions about the feasibility of creating a UK 'national water grid'. More realistically, exports of Welsh water could increase as drier weather and over-abstraction from rivers and aquifers in southern England take their toll. Certainly such exports would bring money into Wales. (For the record, Wales, excluding waters diverted east after regulation of the rivers Severn and Wye, piped almost 430 billion litres to England in 1991, almost fifty per cent of Wales' total output. This makes water Wales' most important resource and export, and a phenomenal 'bargain' for English metropolitan districts.)

The prospect of more drowned valleys is also one of social and environmental conflict. The sound of chapel bells beneath the macadam-like surface of our reservoirs still haunts the Welsh psyche. As we have seen, water is a major export, yet twenty-five per cent of it escapes through leaking mains. What price the construction of another reservoir when a whole reservoir's worth is lost every year? In the next century, it is highly probable that the shortage of water in such areas as the Middle East will be the cause of warfare or unexpected alliances. In Wales, plans for another Tryweryn, Clywedog or even a Graig Goch would foster real links between the currently diverse groupings that practice their politics outside the ossified party system.

Undoubtedly our water environments are of immense importance to the way we, and others, perceive our country. The Welsh coastline of 1,200 kilometres contains some of the most dramatic and unspoiled of European landscapes. We also boast over 5,000 kilometres of rivers, which include certain of the cleanest and most scenically impressive in the UK.

Yet our marine- and fresh-waters continue to act as a depository for vast amounts of toxic and embarrassing waste. The sewage of seventy-five per cent of the Welsh population ends up in our seas, twenty per cent of the total pumped raw from some of the 230 outfalls between Chepstow and the Dee Estuary. Two million tonnes of sewage sludge are dumped by North-West Water off the North Wales coast every year, a practice that will continue until 1998. Traditional industry is another major abuser of our waters. British Steel at Margam and Llanwern, one of the most significant polluters, is allowed to disgorge almost 1,800 tonnes of oil and grease and 87 tonnes of cyanide each year into the Severn Estuary, which because of discharges from Avonmouth, Barry and other industrial centres, is also a UK 'hotspot' for cadmium, a highly toxic heavy metal. Along our rivers there are an estimated 3,000 storm-water overflows which release raw sewage.

Privatisation of the water industry in Wales was unpopular but drew nothing like the angry mass reaction experienced in Scotland. (Similarities with the Poll Tax are clear here. Yet again we must enquire whether the modern Welsh, compared with past generations, are a politically-neutered race.) Thus since 1990, our entire coastline has effectively been a 'free good' given over to a private concern, Dŵr Cymru Welsh Water, for use as a disposal site for our waste. Such a privilege poses the company a massive credibility problem that its clean-up strategy, no matter how clearly prioritised, is unlikely to solve.

Our insatiable appetite for information has meant that 'environmental' matters such as marine pollution are aired ceaselessly in the media. Whether we purchase a satellite dish or *The Ecologist*, we are tuned in to the daily pillaging of the environment. This in itself is part of our dilemma. We now have no excuses for ignorance of the acidification of Wales, the damage done by opencast mining, the destruction of the Amazon rainforest, the desertification of vast areas of the globe. Yet the information remains meaningless because it is unuseable. Our addiction to information has coincided with, indeed hastened, our depoliticisation. Paralysed by the blizzard of impressions we encounter in the press and television, we sit it out in our domestic bunkers or allow ourselves to be submerged in the rituals of work. And do nothing, because there is clearly nothing we can do that will make a difference. In such a sense, information is a means of disempowerment.

This, naturally, creates guilt. And it is guilt that has created a phenomenon called 'green consumerism'. In less than a decade this has immensely broadened, yet perhaps fatally trivialised, the concepts of 'environmentalism' and 'environmental action'. The suspicion that shopping, and not smoking chimneys, might kill the planet, moved the ethos of Western consumerism and its instinctive desire to export itself into the vast, largely untouched 'markets' of what was the Eastern bloc, Russia, China and the Third World, firmly into the forefront of the public mind. At least for a time. However, the spending classes have become so confused by the hyperbole, contradictions and downright lies of 'eco-friendly marketing' that it might be suggested that green consumerism has already shot its bolt as a major force for environmental good.

Indeed, there are few more enervating sights in our high streets and malls than those remaining stores primarily selling green goods, which themselves are almost lost in a welter of petitions and posters about fox-hunting, homeopathy and Buddhism. True, the major supermarket chains have continued quietly to promote their green lines (it is crucial to see more progress here) and there exists the promise of the long-awaited, glacially-slow EU 'eco-labelling' system. But what we now encounter (at least in public) is very much the dimming afterglow of the explosion in environmental awareness of the late eighties. It cannot be claimed, however, that concerned consumerism has ever had much impact in Wales.

Consumer choice and practice is a matter of lifestyle and education. But we must also ask what state policy promises for Wales. As ever, the environment remains tomorrow's priority, as do pledges for greater public accountability and access to information regarding problem subjects. For example, the Government has now reneged on plans for registers that would have listed many of the estimated 12,000 contaminated land sites in Wales. The 'Earth Summit' with its shopping list of global good intentions has been put into perspective by our Government's White Paper on Energy of 1993. Here was a real opportunity to lay the foundations of a long-term, coherent energy policy that emphasised efficiency, defined sustainable generation and encouraged clean production of indigenous reserves. The chance was not only missed, but cynically avoided.

This is emphasised in the official claim that Value Added Tax must be placed on fuel partly because of a UK commitment to reducing increases in our output of carbon dioxide, the major cause of global warming. Here is a case of the Government simply using the environment as an excuse for inequitable actions. Wales has bitter experience of the climatic irregularity that is thought to be caused by pollution. The storm surges that have recently surprised Newgale and inundated Towyn, Cardigan and Llandudno have left permanent scars.

Yet VAT should only be imposed on fuel after a comprehensive policy for improving domestic energy efficiency has been implemented. Such an increase in fuel costs should be part of a coherent, wide-ranging carbon tax. But at present too many of our homes are energy sieves. A rise in heating costs will mean hardship in Wales and other places possessing old housing stock and where average income is below the UK norm. Moreover, about nineteen per cent of the Welsh population consists of old age pensioners — a figure that rises to a startling thirty per cent in some coastal resorts.

INTRODUCTION

The welcome given to VAT charges by some of the country's most well-respected pressure groups is further proof that a uniform UK campaigning style that ignores national, regional and social differences, merely damages the environmental cause. The fact that there is no pledge that the revenues gained from VAT charges will go towards energy efficiency projects is a further reason for opposing this bogusly green extension of the tax.

However, one of the few welcome components of our new energy 'strategy' is the cutting of UK opencast coal production by twenty-five per cent by 1998. Yet there is no promise that opencasting will decline in Wales. Rather, there appears the likelihood that the South Wales coalfield could become a national opencast ghetto, and that we will continue to be the incredulous victims of British Coal propaganda that this form of mining, the ugly child of wartime emergency and post-war austerity, actually enhances the landscape. Certainly the community opposition to opencasting will grow in strength. Wales Against Opencast is one of the largest single issue environmental lobbies in Wales and a good example of English- and Welsh-speaking communities uniting in common cause.

Of great significance has been the rapid evolution of the arguments of such groups. Knee-jerk, not-in-my-back-yard reactions are now leavened with sophisticated information on local authority targets to reduce emissions of warming gases, and the urgency of adopting rigorous energy efficiency standards. This combination of personal, sometimes angry involvement and national, even global data indicates how to ensure campaigns are as effective as possible. The problem remains that too few protesters are capable of interpreting available information and using it to place opencasting in its energy context. Meanwhile, the purchase and deliberate destruction by British Coal of houses in Welsh-speaking areas (in advance of planning applications) remains one of the worst environmental scandals of this country.

The ancient challenges to the environment must be considered afresh by the movements that claim to hold its interests at heart. Environmentalists therefore need to convince previously uncontacted sections of the public that working-class men do not necessarily have to die prematurely of heart disease; that any job is not inevitably better than no job; and that allowing the majority of our children to leave school untutored in nutrition, craft skills and environmental responsibility is nothing to be proud of. These are difficult new fields for organisations used to campaigning on clear-cut threats posed by quarrying, sewage in seawater, or nuclear energy. But if environmentalism is to remain a popular and politically-influential priority, such development must occur.

The question of work is especially important here. Oil and gas exploration around Wales has been greeted by local councils and media as an inevitable jobs bonanza for unemployment blackspots such as Milford, Pembroke Dock, Cardigan and Llŷn. This has occurred without a shred of evidence being provided that hydrocarbon finds will bring lasting benefits to communities and not simply another boom, another bust. Moreover, drilling has always been welcomed when there is as yet no way of assessing what impact it might have on tourism.

This is another industry that brings its own environmental blight, but one which can be managed more sustainably, despite the difficulties in reaching any overall definition of a phenomenon that has tremendous influence over the landscapes and cultures of Wales. The question of impact is especially important in Gwynedd, where almost forty per cent of the £1.3 billion that tourism brings into the Welsh economy each year, is spent.

Yet how to involve more people in environmentalism remains our major challenge. To its detriment, the subject for most of us is a bewildering lobscouse of unrelated ingredients, ranging from campaigning for better street-lighting in intimidating urban areas, to guarding the nests of red kites. (Not that 'environmentalism' is, in itself, an answer to anything, as Alwyn Jones illustrates later in this volume.) One problem has been that the 'issues' have become more confusing, as obvious, black-smoke-from-filthy-chimney-type pollution declines. Gone is the 'smokeless fuel' plant from Abercwmboi, once surely the perfect location for a film of *Hard Times*. Hidden also is much of the poisoned desert into which industry has turned the lower Swansea valley. Today it is much more difficult to comprehend the equally dangerous, yet less visible threats posed by chemicals, radiation and genetic engineering. We should also note the confusion created by the self-administered green gloss of the business world.

The triumph of image over reality is most clearly expressed in the activities of those companies which claim to enhance the environment whilst actually destroying it. Well publicised green stunts and sponsorship deals allow the ugly truths of pollution of air and water, land destruction and toxic waste dumping to become, to borrow a verb used by John Pilger, 'normalised'. In short, the unacceptable becomes the unremarkable.

Environmental organisations should realise that sponsorship of their work has its price. That there is no such thing as a free lunch is a maxim yet to be learned by many. For a pittance offered for deals over tree planting programmes or publications fees, these groups provide the polluters with priceless green publicity. But before we criticise we should consider why organisations such as wildlife trusts are forced to make their Faustian bargains.

The answer is simply because not enough Welsh people feel sufficiently bothered about their local environment to pay a subscription fee. Without money, even the most well-motivated group is impotent. Thus apathy or the loss of political sensibility are the public moods that industry finds most conducive to its triumph in normalising what should always be perceived as abnormal and insupportable.

To help us overcome this, we should identify our best allies. Therefore it is important that those who work for the sustainability of our rural and urban worlds should recognise that in the literatures of Wales we possess a magnificent body of proof for the inspirational, ever-changing yet eternal qualities of the Welsh environment. Dafydd ap Gwilym, Waldo Williams, Glyn Jones, and Roland Mathias might be better campaign friends than the Welsh Office Digest of Environmental Statistics or print-outs from the National Rivers Authority. And so might the songwriters for Welsh-language rock groups or our increasing number of innovative drama companies.

Indeed, there are a multitude of ways we can work and most of them can be taught to us by women. Our environment will continue to suffer unnecessarily until both sexes are fairly represented in politics and industry. The painfully chafing irony here, of course, is that there is only one female contributor to *Green Agenda*.

I can assure the reader this damning imbalance has occurred despite the best efforts of the editor. My only explanation is that in most cases where women have risen to influential positions in the Welsh environmental movement, they have done so in organisations that avoid polemics and eschew political debate. Controversy is unwelcome because it corrodes grant-aid. As to the position of women writers in Wales, we have a hugely talented collection of poets and children's fiction writers. In Elaine Morgan, we possess a fine author of ideas. But there is a damaging shortage of essayists and intelligent journalists. This is all the more disappointing when it is remembered that in many of the more radical Welsh organisations, women supply most of the administrative and intellectual energies.

Certainly we require greater female influence to ensure that the stewardship of the environment (an interesting phrase, once coined for Margaret Thatcher) must not be allowed to pass by default to factions that see only a fragment of the picture. These are the private companies such as Dŵr Cymru, statutory 'watchdogs' like the Countryside Council for Wales, which on an issue such as off-shore hydrocarbon exploration is firmly confined to kennel, or the emerging priesthood of computer-literate, well-resourced, home-based activists who are now replacing the old-style pressure group cells. Local government, which has enormous environmental influence, is crying out for able women to help modernise its image as a depository for third-rate male politicians and quiet-life male bureaucrats.

It must also be realised that there exists a breed of activist alienated from the mainstream, which considers the usual pressure-group tactics of letter-writing and council lobbying as pointless or even collaborationist. Its assessment of our environmental plight has meant a use of the tactics of non-violent direct action and civil resistance. These activists, who bring a welcome freshness to the stuffy environmental establishment, will have an increasing part to play in how the public perceives green issues. Indeed, a sizeable minority now feel that only the martyrdom imparted by imprisonment for physically opposing unnecessary developments in areas vital to the spiritual, cultural and environmental integrity of Wales, will instigate meaningful change.

Here, of course, they have a good deal to learn from *Cymdeithas yr Iaith*, which, itself showing signs of exhaustion, would also benefit from such cross-fertilisation. (The *Cymdeithas* direct action tactics of wall-daubing and office-trashing have developed a puerility through repetition. The organisation requires a major rethink.) Managed carefully, a coalition of language activists, green campaigners and those who acknowledge the inevitability of Wales assuming democratic political responsibility for its own affairs, could have a major stake in how our present quangoland is run.

Ensuring that 'environmentalism' is a genuine priority for everyone is now one of the most pressing challenges for the health and education services of Wales. As to our politicians, there persists the grave suspicion that their lack of knowledge betrays a fundamental dearth of interest in this matter. But even devolution of power in Wales poses environmental threats. It is interesting to speculate how a Welsh *senedd* with its inevitable core of party yes-men and stalwart councillors nominated for seats as testimonials to loyalty, would cope with the blandishments of big business wishing to exploit oil and gas around our coasts; water, coal and other minerals ashore; or further develop Wales as a tourist destination.

Yet perhaps above all we should occasionally stop and consider how lucky we are. John Barnie elsewhere in this volume touches on the subject of population growth and its massive contribution to environmental degradation. Yet although there are movements which for many years have given prominence to the idea that the UK is over-populated, it is difficult to apply that argument to Wales, despite the staggering transformation of the once sparsely-peopled southern valleys in less than two hundred years. (Perhaps I am badly at fault here but my personal assessment is that the Welsh over-population crisis concerns 13 million sheep, and the subsequent over-grazing of our hills and moors.) Depopulation of Welsh speaking areas must also be described as environmentally corrosive.

However, looking at what is occurring in Latin America, India and the Far East, it can be confidently claimed that the 'environmental holocaust' long proclaimed by science-fiction writers and once-discredited doomtellers, has already begun. It has been instigated for generations on a global scale by combination of poverty, exploitation and stupendous Western over-consumption, and is now deliberately exacerbated by the greatest source for social and environmental evil ever devised. This is Third World debt and the impossibility of ever settling even the interest on the account. The blame for this lies with the International Monetary Fund and the World Bank, but also at every cash-point and counter of our friendly, neighbourhood bank branches. It is no overstatement to compare our own computer-reckoned monthly financial state-ments to epitaphs for children of the 'developing' world. Every digit digs a grave.

Of course, whatever the state of our beaches or the quality of our air, that holocaust is almost undetectable in Wales. It may well remain so for many years, such is Western skill at turning a deaf ear to the human tragedy of much of the Third World. (A skill, some might argue, not nearly so well honed as that for ignoring the rights and opinions of your own minorities and underclass.)

I write that in the knowledge that the Re-Chem plant near Pontypool appears responsible for some of the worst PCB pollu-tion in the UK; that the pressure to keep our aged Magnox nuclear reactors running has revealed the desperation and greed of indus-trial short-termism at its worst; and that there exist big businesses in this country which routinely place profit before the protection of human health. I am also aware that by UK standards, there are pockets of life-denying poverty to be found in Wales. Yet the truth is that insulated as most of us are by relative wealth and an environment that for all its problems, is, by Third World terms, fairly well regulated, if not protected, many of us will be among the last people on the planet to feel personally and unavoidably affected by the crisis which, whether in the rainforest or the thoroughfares of great cities, already appears unstoppable.

Robert Minhinnick

Dr Phil Williams

UK Energy Policy and the Welsh Environment

Introduction: the World Scenario

Twenty years ago the Club of Rome published a report on the future of the Earth called 'Limits of Growth'. The basic thesis was that if the population of the Earth kept rising, and if the raw materials consumed annually on average by each person kept rising, then eventually the non-renewable resources of the world would be exhausted and the level of pollution would rise to dangerous levels. A secondary argument pointed out that as easily-won resources were exhausted poorer-grade raw materials would be exploited: these would require a higher input of energy for extraction and cause more pollution, so there was a potentially fatal positive feedback.

'Limits of Growth' constructed various models of the future based on different assumptions. Most of the models led to worldwide catastrophe when the sharp fall in available resources coincided with the need to exploit lower-grade minerals and to control rising population — both demanding more resources. A significant feature of these models was that the 'standard of living' would still be rising when the situation was already beyond the point of no return and catastrophe was inevitable.

'Limits of Growth' was attacked on many grounds. For example, it underestimated the level of undiscovered resources — but this

23

was a criticism of the *timing* of the models, not the *basic principle*. Exponential growth dominates in the end — and the end comes sooner than people expect.

A second criticism was that the free market would control the use of resources, so that as a raw material became scarce, the price would rise and use would be curtailed or a substitute found.

However, this is a naïve view of the free market. When I gave seminars on 'The Limits of Growth' in the 1970s, I invented a raw material called Ultimum. It occurred in two places and was exploited by two firms in fierce competition. The actual cost of extraction and distribution was low, and to preserve market share both firms had to sell the product at a low price. If either firm increased the price unilaterally, it would lose the market and the shareholders would receive no profit. So both firms continued to sell at a low price until simultaneously both mines were totally exhausted.

I was presenting a rather simple and hypothetical model of free market competition. Nowadays there is no need for a hypothetical model since oil production follows my model exactly. In real terms petrol is cheaper now than when I bought my first car thirty years ago. The opening of the North Sea and Alaskan oil fields — both relatively small — created a small surplus on the world market. OPEC fell apart as several producers refused to cut production. So the price fell.

This fall in oil price has nothing to do with any great increase in known reserves. It is still probable that oil reserves will be exhausted within the lifetime of today's teenage joyrider. If market forces were to ensure the permanent availability of oil, prices should *already* be rising sharply. The low price of oil is a simple demonstration that the free market is totally unable to ensure the long-term security of essential raw materials. The plan to use North Sea gas to generate electricity is another example.

The basic thesis of 'Limits of Growth' is therefore vindicated, and oil and gas illustrate the different aspects of the thesis in a very significant way — both the exhaustion of reserves and the increase in pollution.

The exhaustion of traditional energy supplies will profoundly alter the economic and political balance in the world and undermine the hegemony of the present industrial powers. At the same time the generation of power poses the most serious threat to the environment of our planet.

Of these two threats it is the damage to the environment which now seems most urgent. The most obvious example of environmental damage is the acidification of rainfall. Dying trees and sterile lakes are undeniable evidence of the environmental cost of 'cheap' power, and as 'Limits of Growth' predicted, as resources are exhausted the level of pollution will increase. The threat of orimulsion, a cheap, sulphur-rich fuel imported into the UK from Venezuela, illustrates the thesis only too well.

However, there is an even more serious environmental threat. The burning of fossil fuels plus the felling of rainforests is causing a steady increase in the carbon dioxide content of the atmosphere (three per cent per decade). Over a hundred years ago Arrhenius predicted that such an increase would, through the greenhouse effect, cause an increase in average global temperature. The evidence suggests that this is now occurring. The last ten years have included several of the hottest years since global records began.

Many factors control weather and they are inter-related in such a complex way that no-one can predict global warming with any precision. The oceans play a vital role in absorbing and distributing carbon dioxide and in buffering the rise in temperature. There is positive feedback from the release of greenhouse gases trapped in the tundra — and negative feedback from accelerated plant growth. Above all, water vapour in the atmosphere is decisive; yet at lower heights it is a greenhouse gas, trapping heat, as can be observed on a cloudy night in winter, while at greater heights water is an anti-greenhouse gas, reflecting incident radiation before it reaches the lower atmosphere.

If the *degree* of warming is uncertain, the *consequences* are even more uncertain. A rise in sea level and the flooding of coastal areas are virtually certain. So is an increase in the number and ferocity of cyclones. But the changes in the general weather pattern are less predictable. A possible irony is that Wales could actually become colder as strong warming of the polar regions affects the prevailing south-westerly winds and hence alters the Gulf Stream. The safest prediction is that weather patterns would change significantly, and the traditional patterns of agriculture in many regions of the world would become invalid. Sheep farmers don't become experts at wine-making nor do wine-makers know much about the care of camels.

So far no honest scientist can be absolutely certain, and the confident, complacent statements by 'scientists' representing oil or coal companies can be dismissed. Nevertheless there is a broad consensus of leading meteorologists who accept the evidence for an increase in mean global temperature and warn of possible catastrophic changes in climate. They also agree that by the time they are absolutely certain it will be too late. With such evidence the pressure for international action to control the emission of carbon dioxide is growing.

Stabilising the emission from industrialised nations at the 1990 level is totally inadequate. This is the emission that is already creating a greenhouse effect, and if the rest of the world emulates the West and demands an equal level of industrialisation then there is little hope. If China produces 1,000 million tonnes of coal a year, increasingly for home consumption, stabilising European carbon dioxide emission at 1990 levels will have negligible effect. International agreement must balance the demand that Third World countries preserve their rainforests and severely limit their use of fossil fuels, with a corresponding demand for industrialised countries to reduce sharply their emission of carbon dioxide.

This is not an easy demand for the West to meet. We have a strong addiction to energy and a sudden cut in our power consumption will be extremely disrupting and unpopular. It may need more than the uncertain predictions of scientists to persuade us to make the sacrifice. However, powerful evidence for the scientific case comes from other forms of pollution that can no longer be denied. The ozone hole is a serious threat in itself, but its main significance may be to persuade ordinary people that if something as trivial and everyday as a CFC spray can actually damage the atmosphere over the whole Earth, it is quite plausible that the massive output of power stations and cars can cause even greater damage.

As mentioned above, this has already been demonstrated in the case of acid rain. Without adequate cleaning of exhaust, the sulphur dioxide produced in burning many kinds of coal or oil acidifies the rain and this destroys forests and sterilises lakes and rivers throughout the world. There may still be arguments about the exact proportions that different countries contribute to the withering of German forests, the sterilisation of Scandinavian lakes and the poisoning of Welsh rivers — and the relative proportions caused by power stations or by cars, but there is no longer any doubt that international pressure will soon forbid the burning of coal and oil without adequate cleaning of the exhaust, and that this will add substantially to the cost of power generation from fossil fuel, especially from coal, and also put severe restrictions on the design of cars. But this will not end the environmental impact: the steps necessary to clean the exhaust from power stations will themselves lead to a massive increase in limestone quarrying.

If there is any virtue in the more obvious forms of pollution, it is that they may educate people to recognise the underlying problem of energy. These factors are setting the scenario for the next decade and it is certain that the present reliance on burning fossil fuels will no longer be possible. We need a firm plan to halve our output of carbon dioxide, with the reduction shared about equally between energy conservation and substitution of alternative sources of power for oil, gas and coal.

But the Western world will still need to be persuaded to take such a radical step. There needs to be a large-scale pilot scheme to prove that energy consumption can be reduced without the quality of life being impaired, and that alternative sources of power can be reliable and economic.

If God designed one spot on Earth that was perfect for that pilot scheme it was Wales. Built on a foundation of coal, with a coastline exposed to the waves of the Atlantic and punctuated by estuaries that funnel the tides to record heights, and with windswept moorlands from which a fan of rivers flow to the sea, Wales is an ideal laboratory for comparing most forms of energy generation. And in this comparison we can also include the longest experience of large-scale fission power.

In fact, most of the necessary ingredients for a pilot scheme exist in Wales already — but piecemeal with no overall planning, no major research back-up and on too small a scale. What is needed is a government with plans that stretch beyond the next election and with the imagination to drive a major long-term project.

Unfortunately, we suffer a government whose energy policies can be summed up entirely in one sentence: "the future can be left to the free market". Now the free market may be very good for producing car-phones or video cameras, but, as argued above, it is inadequate to cope with long-term programmes. The control of global pollution can never be a high priority to the accountants in a free-market enterprise. Even Adam Smith did not believe the free market could solve everything — perhaps because he lived in a city already suffering from smoke pollution.

When I was asked to write on Government Energy Policy I felt that this was like writing on mountaineering in Flanders. So instead I have assumed that Wales were governed by a far-sighted administration. What energy policies would be possible? And which of them would serve our long-term interest?

An Energy Budget for Wales

The root cause of the problem is the ever-growing demand for energy as today's luxury becomes tomorrow's necessity. When I was a child I spent every August in a farm in Gwynfe where there was no electricity supply; it colours my attitude to the 'necessities' of modern life that I remember those summers with great hiraeth. In the 1960s the last farms in Wales were connected to the grid. Now, undoubtedly, they share with the rest of us the 'need' for electric fires and storage heaters, washing machines and tumble driers, refrigerators and deep-freezers, computers and colour televisions.

In fact the annual consumption of electricity in Wales has increased from less than 1 TWh (Terawatt-hours or 1,000,000,000 kiloWatt-hours) before the war, to about 3 TWh in 1950, 12 TWh in 1970 and about 15 TWh today — 5,000 kiloWatt-hours per person or an average continuous use of 600 Watts per person. The first step in any energy plan is to reduce this figure, and with quite moderate policies total consumption could be cut by twenty-five per cent before the year 2010 without anyone feeling any hardship or discomfort.

Energy Conservation

The technology already exists to cut power consumption without loss in comfort or facilities. For example, space heating accounts for about thirty per cent of our energy use; yet proper insulation of houses, offices and factories can reduce this demand to well under half the present level.

To a serious extent Wales suffers from a history of cheap fuel. When I was growing up in Bargoed, all miners received a very generous supply of free coal and a flourishing back-lane trade distributed the surplus to non-mining families. Roaring coal fires in more than one room, kept burning all day, were normal. Not surprisingly, insulation was given low priority. I can still remember the pleasure of walking down Wood Street on a cold day and feeling the glow of heat as I passed the end house of each terrace. Many of the houses are still without adequate insulation, but the days of free coal for half the population are long gone.

More surprising is the lack of insulation in modern buildings. I work in a university physics department with an impressive area of single-glazed window where there is no network of temperature monitors to control the distribution of heat through the building. Last year we introduced a course on Energy and the Environment and one of our first projects was to study our overall use of energy — literally to put our own house in order.

A target to ensure deep loft insulation, adequate draught-proofing and multiple-glazing for all existing and new buildings by the year 2010 is not utopian. If it rapidly pays an individual like myself to carry out these improvements in my own home it must surely pay society to do the same for *all* homes.

The economic benefits will not only be measured in reduced energy consumption. The transformation will create increased employment in the building industry at a time when it is severely depressed, and the work will be widely distributed and carried out by many small companies so that benefit will be felt in every town and village. It will also create a demand for petro-chemical, glass and aluminium products — all produced in Wales.

The balance sheet is rosy. The only problem is political. To ensure that all houses are properly insulated would require one hundred per cent grants for low-income families. An argument I have heard against such a scheme is that it would be 'unfair' on those individuals like myself who have already spent their own money on insulation. My answer is simple: I have already recouped the money I have spent on insulation through lower fuel bills, and if State capital can now be used to spread the benefits to every home in Wales, rather than used to build new nuclear power stations, I will be perfectly happy.

I can see a more tricky problem in reducing the total demand for space heating in commercial and industrial premises. Here a stick-and-carrot approach may be necessary with generous grants to enable firms to meet increasingly stringent standards.

With political will we could be enjoying major benefits long before 2010 — but even that is too long-term for the present government and the budget for energy conservation is contracting. According to the Association for the Conservation of Energy, in recent years the sale of energy-saving items like double-glazing and loft insulation has fallen sharply — more evidence that the free market is failing to tackle the long-term problem.

Better insulation and the use of heat exchangers would also make a dramatic improvement in the energy efficiency of most domestic appliances. The average refrigerator in Wales today is estimated to consume 270 kWh per annum. The combination of slim-line styling to fit the 'modern' kitchen, with penny-pinching economies on sealing and door catches, mean that refrigerators today are less efficient than those in use 20 years ago. Yet another triumph of the free market. However, the best on general sale in the shops consume only 80 kWh per annum, and for 'state-of-the-art' models this has been cut to 40 kWh per annum — almost a sevenfold improvement. A similar improvement is possible for freezers where the average in use consumes 530 kWh per annum which the best design can reduce to 100 kWh per annum.

Lighting is another area where common practice is woefully inadequate. It is possible to buy a 20 W bulb with the same light output as a 100 W tungsten-wire bulb, yet recently in Wales, in a shop which sold nothing except electric lights, I found only one rather clumsy, out-of-date low-energy bulb on sale. In the USA, under pressure of legislation, electricity companies are obliged to encourage conservation and in some cases they have distributed low-energy fluorescent light bulbs free of charge. Yet such a policy seems unthinkable in present-day Wales: such is the measure of our indifference to the energy problem.

Television sets also use far more energy than necessary. Indeed it is estimated that if high-resolution television is introduced using present technology, the total power demand in Europe will increase by an amount larger than the whole power generated at present in the UK. Yet an alternative, low-power technology already exists — and I am using it to write this essay on my notebook computer.

This is an area where the scope for government action is relatively straightforward. It is already illegal to sell dangerous products: similar legislation could prevent the sale of products that waste energy. As a very modest first step it should be compulsory for all electric products to be prominently labelled according to their energy efficiency.

Policies to conserve electricity are the easiest to introduce as they offer the major attraction of equivalent or improved comfort and facility at lower cost, and the benefits are apparent within a year or so.

At the same time, I am conscious that the second largest user of energy is transport. No energy policy can be successful unless we can eliminate the present dependence on car travel. Here there are two developments which must be given the highest priority, to be completed before the first major oil-crisis of the next century.

The simplest, cheapest and quickest way to reduce car travel is to make it unnecessary. Here, I must give credit to the University of Wales. At present, I give two post-graduate tutorials a year to students in Cardiff and Swansea — but the only travelling involved is a cycle-ride to the video-link studio in Llanbadarn. I also use it about four times a year to take part in committee meetings.

One of the most important developments I would advocate for the next fifteen years is the establishment of a video and data communication network with optic fibres connected to every office and home. Long-distance commuting to work in an office will become obsolescent. A version of this, which will preserve the social dimension of work, will be the establishment of village communication centres where a number of people can work together in the same building. As it happens, this also has the special economic benefit for Wales that on Deeside we have one of the most advanced centres for the development of optic fibre technology.

However, some travel will always be necessary and another priority must be an efficient, comfortable, reliable and cheap sys-

tem of public transport serving the whole of Wales. This is properly discussed under transport policy, but no energy policy can be
complete without assuming that at some time early in the next
century there will be a network of electrified railways serving
every major community in Wales. In the 1960s it was already a
debating point that Wales generated a huge surplus of electricity
but did not have a single mile of electrified railways. In the 1990s
it is a scandal. The capital costs of such a network would be far
higher than the cost of a conservation programme or the cost of a
fibre-optic network, and the economic benefits will only appear
over a longer period of time. However, the first steps in planning
such a network need to be taken now. New routes — including a
line from Caernarfon to Caerfyrddin — must be identified and
given planning protection, and a timetable for electrification published, beginning with the heavily used lines in the Valleys and
along the north and south coasts.

With reasonable determination between now and the year 2010
it will be possible to cut electricity consumption for all present use
in Wales by thirty-five to forty per cent and then an extra ten to
fifteen per cent could be allocated to meeting new demands,
including electrified railways. This sets a realistic target for electricity consumption in Wales of 11 TWh per annum — an overall
cut of twenty-five per cent over fifteen years.

Energy Generation

The other side of a balanced and sustainable energy budget for
Wales is the generation of power by alternative, non-polluting and
renewable methods. Wales is ideally situated to take a leading part
in the development of the new technologies. Our geographical
location, with a long and exposed coast-line facing the Atlantic,
combined with the research facilities of the University of Wales, a
major steel and aluminium industry, and a tradition of heavy
engineering going back two hundred years, offer us a unique
opportunity.

With an immediate start on a major programme of research,
development and construction, by 2010 alternative methods of
generation could provide 4 TWh per annum, just over a third of

our total consumption, with a complementary capacity of conventional power stations and pump storage schemes to allow quick response to fluctuating demand and fluctuations in wind and tide.

To meet this target of alternative electricity generation requires a mix of methods providing a maximum capacity of about 2 GW (1 Gigawatt = 1 million kilowatts). As a rough indication this would require equal contributions from fifty wind-farms, with an average installed capacity of 8 MW, a sequence of fifteen to twenty tide-race or estuary generators,with an average capacity of about 30 MW, and a chain of off-shore wind and wave generators across Cardigan Bay.

It is important that the public gets a feel for the proper scale of these developments. Propaganda from both sides can be misleading. On the one hand, the more naïve elements in the green movement have presented an image of a village, with the square full of people — all smiling like in an old-style Co-op advertisement — and on the hill a single, small and very pretty windmill which is presumably meeting all the needs of this utopian community. Once you do the sums you realise that one wind turbine falls far short of doing that — not to mention providing a surplus to meet the power needs of Splott, Uplands or Gurnos.

On the other hand, the opponents of alternative energy present a picture of the whole landscape in every direction covered by obtrusive and noisy generators.

The sums give a balanced picture. There is no doubt that if we are to rely extensively on alternative energy then we are dealing with relatively low power densities and we will have to dedicate a fair amount of land to wind-farms — but this means a few per cent rather than fifty per cent. In other words, wind-farms would occupy more land than coal mines or nuclear power stations with equivalent power capacity, but far less than allocated at present for conifer forests or for military purposes.

Wind-Power

The basic unit for wind-power is the wind turbine, where sails or blades rotate in the wind. The design has advanced substantially from the traditional four-sailed model, used to pump water or grind corn. The modern two- or three-blade version is more slender but far more efficient. However, there is a theoretical maximum to the power that can be delivered by a wind turbine. The absolute maximum might seem to be the total energy of the wind passing through the area swept out by the blades. However, the wind must flow away from the blade, carrying energy with it, and it can be shown that the maximum power that can be extracted by the windmill is only fifty-nine per cent of the energy of the wind. In reality, modern windmills can achieve eighty per cent of this theoretical maximum, so if the area swept out by the blades is A square metres and the wind is blowing at v metres per second then the total power generated by each windmill is equal to $0.30 \, A \, v^3$ Watts.

In other words, if we have a highly efficient multi-blade windmill with blades fifteen metres long, operating in a strong breeze (10 metres per second) it will deliver about 220 kW. Thirty-six of these will provide 8 MW. Or, taking arithmetic to its limit, 6,000 of these operating continually in a strong breeze, would generate about 11 TWh per annum.

Unfortunately, reality is not so favourable. As the formula shows the power varies as the cube of the wind speed, so if the wind drops to a moderate breeze (5 metres per second) the power output drops to under 30 kW — and at this level it would require 44,000 windmills to meet our total demand! And of course, when the air was entirely calm there would be no power at all.

An alternative is to build much bigger windmills. The biggest in Britain on Burger Hill in Orkney has thirty metre blades and in a strong breeze can generate over 1 MW; but in calm conditions it is as ineffective as the smallest machine.

This v-cubed factor is the main objection to a total dependence on wind-power. In the long term it would be reasonable to provide about twenty per cent of total power demand, but in a plan for the next fifteen years it would be more realistic to assume a maximum of fifty wind-farms, with an average of about fifty turbines per farm, producing a total of about 1 TWh per annum — or just under ten per cent of our reduced demand in 2010. These wind-farms would occupy just over one per cent of the total agricultural land of Wales, and of course the land around each tower would still be used for agriculture with the rental from the generating company providing extra income for the farmer.

Although support from the non-fossil fuel obligation will be less in future, windfarms are already becoming economically competi-tive, and we might predict that the initial developments in Lland-inam, Cemaes and Trefenter will be copied. There is, however, one important factor which may restrict the total number of projects.

The early wind-farms have caused considerable local opposi-tion. The NIMBY objections I think we can safely ignore — esp-ecially from those who have come to Wales to find a 'better environment'. If their rural idyll is at the expense of global pollu-tion, or a PWR nuclear reactor somewhere else, then their hypocrisy should be challenged. (There is a story, probably apoc-ryphal, that in one case a wife arranged an evening protest meeting at her home. Her husband — who supported wind-farms — waited until the meeting had assembled and then collected all the fuses and drove off so that the meeting could appreciate a world without electricity.)

Technical objections to the noise of wind-generators must be considered but here there is ground for optimism. An improved profile for the trailing edges of the blades can reduce noise and improve performance. Noisy gear-boxes are simply bad design and should be prohibited.

The most serious mistake, however, has been the failure to involve the community in a substantial share of the ownership and management of the wind-farms. It is easy to see wind-farms as the latest chapter in a history of exploitation where the natural re-sources of Wales have created great wealth but brought little benefit to the people of Wales.

I have recently been reading a history of Scandinavia. At the turn of the century capitalists had bought a large number of waterfalls in Norway. After independence in 1905, however, the 'Concession Laws' were passed which applied State control over the use of waterfalls, with the law insisting that all waterfalls with dams should eventually become State property. Hydro-electricity is now a major benefit to the people of Norway, and any Government plan must ensure that wind-power does the same for Wales.

Tidal Generators

If wind speed is unreliable, tides are entirely reliable and can be predicted years in advance. Drawing energy from the gravitational potential of the Moon, tides offer a source of power that can be sustained for astronomical periods of time.

The principle of tidal barrages is very simple: a barrage is built on the estuary of a river and at high tide the barrage is opened to allow the estuary to fill with water. The barrage is then closed, and at low tide the head of water is used to generate electricity. In some designs both the inflow of water on the rising tide and the outflow are used. Nevertheless, tidal generators can only operate for a fraction of the day so their average output can only be about twenty-five to thirty per cent of the peak.

World-wide, tidal power is of limited potential, but Wales is one of the favoured locations. The tide in the Atlantic is funnelled into the Irish Sea and then funnelled again into the Severn Estuary and Liverpool Bay. The tidal reach in the Severn is, in fact, claimed as the second highest in the world. Another favourable feature of the Welsh coastline is that there is a time lag of several hours between high tide at Milford Haven and high tide at Hoylake, so the semi-diurnal variation of output from a single station can be largely balanced throughout the grid.

The best-known tidal generator is the 240 MW station at La Rance in Brittany. Despite its success, no tidal barrages have been built in the UK. As far back as 1947 F.O. Harber published feasibility studies for eight tidal power stations in North Wales alone, but none of these have ever been built. There are several reasons for this.

The first is shared with all techniques for harnessing natural energy: the fuel may be free, and the running costs low, but the capital costs are high; and whereas a wind-farm can be developed in stages, the whole capital expense of a tidal barrage must be met at the outset before a single Watt of power is generated.

The second objection arises from a genuine clash of environmental considerations. The effects of a barrage on wildlife, and on the shipping and fishing interests in the estuary are uncertain. Unfortunately, most attention has been focused on two very large projects: one at the mouth of the Mersey and the other across the Severn Estuary. The Severn Estuary barrage offers the possibility of generating seven per cent of the present electricity demand of the UK — or about twice the power demand proposed for Wales in 2010. But in proportion to the attraction of a single renewable source meeting all our energy needs are the environmental uncertainties and the commercial interests affected.

However, it seems a pity to abandon consideration of a form of energy generation that is so totally reliable and so totally sustainable and which does no harm to the global environment whatever effects it may have in the immediate locality. An energy plan for Wales should therefore consider a number of small-scale schemes which will serve as test projects, operating for several years before any major barrage is seriously considered.

A typical small-scale project is the one proposed for the Conwy, with 30 MW of installed capacity and an annual output of 60 GWh. A sequence of fifteen projects on this scale would match the proposed fifty wind-farms in generating about ten per cent of our projected energy demand. Distributed along the coast of Wales they would take advantage of the different times of high tide to provide a guaranteed base-load of power. On some estuaries such a barrage would offer the additional advantage of a road-crossing.

In assessing the environmental effect of such schemes it must be remembered that the flooded area at high tide is effectively unchanged, but of course when the station is actually generating the level of water changes much more rapidly than usual. This will require special provision for boats using the estuary. These are factors that can only be properly assessed when at least one barrage scheme has been completed.

It is also worth adding that of F.O. Harber's eight schemes one harnessed the tidal flow though the Menai Straits rather than in an estuary. Another strong tidal flow occurs between Enlli and Penllyn. To harness tidal flow it is possible to use under-water turbines and these may add to the total power available from the tides in relatively small-scale projects with virtually no adverse environmental effects.

Off-shore Generators

Tidal-flow generators share with off-shore wind turbines and wave-generators the advantage that they promise a renewable power source with the minimum environmental effect.

For off-shore wind turbines the basic technology is the same as on-shore, with the advantage that at a given height above the sea the wind speed will tend to be higher than at a similar height above the land. There are disadvantages, however: problems of corrosion are far worse in the presence of salt spray. Nevertheless as the demand for renewable energy increases, off-shore wind-farms will add considerably to the total generating potential in Wales.

Wave-generators, on the other hand, represent a relatively new technology which could potentially match the contribution from wind and tide. The prototypes developed in Norway have suffered from initial problems, and more development is required before wave power is commercially competitive, but the costs are now dropping. When this technique is mature, however, Wales is ideally placed to harness the energy of the Atlantic waves, and although the incident wave energy varies, it is far more constant than wind energy and is at a maximum in winter when energy needs are highest. The refusal of the Government to continue its very modest financial support for research in this field is one of the clearest indications of its failure to take energy policy seriously.

In an overall fifteen-year energy plan, it is reasonable to expect the initial development of on-shore wind-power to be complete by the year 2000, and a prototype tidal barrage to be generating, perhaps at Conwy. Learning from the experience of the prototype, in the following five years more tidal generators could be constructed and the first off-shore wind turbines. In the final period, leading to the target date of 2010, the introduction of wave-power would be pencilled in so that if the development of this technique is successful it will complete the target of 4 TWh per annum generated by renewable and non-polluting techniques, representing about thirty-five per cent of the reduced electricity demand.

Conventional Energy

The target of an overall cut of 4 TWh in total electricity demand (including an increase of 1.5 TWh in the electricity used for transport) is entirely feasible, provided the Government gives the necessary encouragement.

The target of 4 TWh of power generated by renewable and non-polluting techniques is a more demanding challenge, but it is technically feasible and in the long term economically competitive. The Government has extended the non-fossil fuel obligation, but it still needs to co-ordinate the future development of wind-power, to provide capital grants in support of the prototype tidal generator and the first off-shore wind turbines, and to finance a greatly expanded research programme into wave power. However, the costs will be far smaller than those already allocated to nuclear power with a far greater promise of economic benefit in the long term.

Even so, the gap of 7 TWh will still need to be filled by 'conventional' power stations — just under half the present level. In the medium term, the remaining component of conventional power will offer an important advantage: it will provide quick-response back-up capacity to meet fluctuations in demand and to complement the large fluctuations in the power generated in the alternative sector. So in an all-Wales energy plan, which elements of 'conventional' power will be retained?

It is obvious that it is more difficult to implement an overall energy plan in the privatised sector. It is, for example, quite clear that the Government has been unable to persuade the electricity generating companies to make a large-enough coal burn to reprieve the pits that strong back-bench opinion (supported by overwhelming public opinion) wished to see operating.

The first guess is to assume a fifty per cent cut across the board. With Trawsfynydd closed but Wylfa operating until 2010 this is a reasonable assumption for the nuclear sector.

On the other hand we should certainly seek to expand the present capacity of hydroelectric power. In the days of 'cheap' power it used to be argued that in comparison with Norway and Scotland, the mountains in Wales were not quite high enough to justify many hydroelectric schemes and, unlike France, our rivers were not quite large enough. However, future economics will take far more account of sustainability and environmental costs and it is certain that the role of small-scale hydroelectricity schemes will increase. Moreover, one of the advantages of schemes like Rheidol, Ffestiniog or Llanberis is that the power can be turned on very quickly to match peak demand or a trough in generation.

For power stations burning coal and oil, the future is not so clear. In the past there was an overwhelming argument on social grounds for maintaining the role of deep-mined coal, but it must be remembered that the paramount justification was the need to preserve the communities that depended on coal — not to support coal as such. As I once heard Nye Bevan explain: "We are not moles in Wales that we must have work underground; but we are men and we must have work".

Now that battle is largely lost, the only realistic course is to re-assess the contribution that coal should make, assuming that in future most of the coal will be imported or obtained by opencast mining. The two intrinsic advantages of coal are that the known reserves will last for several hundred years, and that the present generation of coal-fired power stations, using the cheapest imported or opencast coal and burned in old power stations without desulphurisation, provide electricity at the lowest price.

However, these advantages are more than offset by the environmental factors. To start with, opencast mining has a dreadful effect on the local environment and the damage it inflicts on neighbouring villages is intolerable. Even in areas of high unemployment, opposition to opencast schemes is growing.

The environmental damage continues when the coal is burned. In producing a kWh of electricity, coal generates more carbon dioxide than any other fossil fuel, and so contributes most to the greenhouse effect. In addition, coal burning with the present generation of power stations produces an unacceptable level of acid emission, and it is increasingly obvious that this is causing acid rain in Wales as well as in Scandinavia. Faced with the evidence of increasing ecological damage, the Government is complacent, and it is clear that HM Inspectorate of Pollution have postponed any decision to order the generators to install flue gas desulphurisation (FGD) or selective catalytic reduction equipment

(SCRE), other than the few already planned. However, acid pollution does not respect international frontiers and it is certain that international pressure will lead to the EU imposing much tougher limits on acid emission. As soon as these are imposed on all power stations, the cost advantage of coal will disappear. At the same time, the measures taken to reduce acid rain will have their own environmental impact, including a massive expansion in limestone quarrying.

To preserve the communities that depended on deep-mined coal until alternative employment was available, the environmental cost might have been worth paying. But once the transfer to imported or opencast coal is complete the special case for coal disappears. It is therefore reasonable to assume that coal-burning stations, such as Aberthaw, will operate on a reduced load to meet peak demand so that the total power generated by coal-burning will be reduced to less than half the present level.

Similar arguments apply to oil-fired stations. At the moment oil is very cheap on the world market. However, oil reserves will run out long before coal and, although oil produces less greenhouse gases per kWh than coal, it is equally guilty of emitting acid exhaust. Therefore the need to fit FGD equipment to meet stringent EU limits will increase the cost of oil-generation to the same extent as with coal. There is, however, one worrying possibility with oil-fired stations such as Pembroke: that towards the end of the century they will be allowed to burn the bitumen-based fuel orimulsion. This must be opposed at all costs.

The answer given by the generating companies, with the tacit support of the Government, is that gas-fired power stations will take over as the main fossil-fuel based power producers. In Wales alone, there are plans for 3.6 GW of installed capacity, partly to take advantage of the gas finds off the North Wales coast.

On the surface, there are two over-riding arguments against using gas for generating electricity. The first is that the North Sea and Liverpool Bay gas fields have a strictly limited lifetime and if gas is allowed to provide the base-load of electricity, it will merely postpone for a short time the need to find an alternative.

The second argument is subtle — yet it is firmly based on a fundamental law of physics, the second law of thermodynamics. A heat engine, such as a turbine in a power station, has a theoretical limit to its maximum efficiency. As a result, Combined Cycle Gas Turbine (CCGT) power stations have an overall efficiency of only fifty per cent. Natural gas, however, has the unique property that it can be burned in a domestic gas fire and deliver almost one hundred per cent of the available energy. It is therefore absurd to burn gas to generate electricity for space heating when the gas could be burned directly with twice the efficiency.

The argument against gas-powered stations is therefore that although they are superior to coal- or oil-fired stations, gas is such a valuable fuel that it is irresponsible to waste its energy content by generating electricity rather than providing primary heat. For this reason, it was once forbidden to burn natural gas to generate electricity, and the second law of thermodynamics still applies. Politicians may change human law but they cannot change the laws of physics.

The real reason for the 'dash-for-gas' is that, without a determined policy to develop alternative sources of power, the Government has no alternative. At the beginning of the 1980s they chose to ignore the warnings of both scientists and economists, and based their energy policy on nuclear fission stations. The combined effect of the Chernobyl accident and the hard-nosed insistence of the private companies that nuclear power was hopelessly uneconomic, left them with no policy at all and the prospect of a serious power gap towards the end of the century. It is the height of cynicism that because the Government have rejected genuine green policies they are forced to present a spurious green justification for CCGT stations.

However, even the most avid enthusiast for gas-fired stations must admit that they only offer a short-term, stop-gap solution, and that by the year 2010 the search for a reliable long-term and non-polluting alternative will be imperative. The greatest danger of the dash-for-gas is that it will allow a complacent and irresponsible Government to postpone the development of alternative energy resources. We must not allow this to happen in Wales: we at least have a duty to the world to take a far-sighted view.

Beyond 2010

As our hypothetical government takes a responsible look beyond 2010, it will be convinced that the role of non-polluting, renewable energy can only increase. Coal will be ruled out on environmental grounds; oil will be expensive and polluting; gas will be exhausted; and nuclear power will be finally exposed as a very expensive and dangerous cover for bomb production. In that context, the energy resources of Wales will be at a premium — provided the necessary development begins now.

The targets I have suggested for the year 2010 are just a first step. Beyond 2010 we must move closer to one hundred per cent dependency on alternative energy and there may be very difficult decisions to be made. Should we approve of the Severn barrage? Will we accept a chain of wind turbines and wave generators stretching from Enlli to St. David's Head?

Without a major programme of research and development over the next fifteen years we will not be equipped to answer those questions.

There is another question we will need to answer if we contemplate one hundred per cent alternative energy. We will no longer be able to rely on quick-response coal-, oil- or gas-fired stations to bridge the gap between unpredictable wind- and wave-power and fluctuating demand. A necessary part of one hundred per cent dependency on alternative energy is the need for storage.

Pump-storage is one possibility but the number of suitable sites in Wales is limited and it is unlikely that pump-storage will be enough. Unless there is an unexpected breakthrough in the design of electric batteries, the most promising medium appears to be hydrogen. Many of the traditional problems of hydrogen — such as safe storage — have been overcome and several car manufacturers are promising hydrogen cars by the end of the century.

But no-one has answered the problem of mass-storage as part of a national electricity-generating system, and here there is an urgent programme of research to be started.

A sustainable supply of non-polluting energy is one of the most important factors in safeguarding our future, yet whatever aspect of the challenge we examine, problems can only be solved by long-term, well-researched Government action.

The potential is exciting, the need is imperative and time is running out. When, oh when, can we begin the job?

Neil Caldwell

Planning for Sustainability

If words were all that mattered, it could be argued that we are on the verge of a new era in planning. The 'let it rip' days of Nicholas Ridley are long gone, and a new framework for land-use planning is steadily being put into place. The way the planning system can be used as an environmental tool to help us build a sustainable society appears to have been recognised. Or has it?

Mr Ridley's dismissal in 1988 halted a process of planning deregulation that had been taking place for most of the decade. A succession of ministers at the Department of the Environment, including Micheal Heseltine, had sought to weaken the planning powers that help to direct and control development, in order, as they put it, "to lift the burden on enterprise". Like so many institutions picked up, examined, then cast to the ground in a neanderthal fashion reminiscent of the ape and the bone in the opening scene of *2001: A Space Odyssey*, the post-war planning system and the consensus which surrounded its operation, was shattered by the Thatcher government.

However, as the decade unfolded, so too did a necklace of battle grounds in Tory-held shires around London, as the volume house-builders and other major developers tried to take advantage by proposing a series of new settlements and out-of-town shopping malls, to the horror of Conservative supporters who objected to 'their countryside' being despoiled by development. These self-confessed 'NIMBYs', so disparaged by the late Mr Ridley, enjoyed the last laugh when they capped some dramatic public inquiry victories by burning an effigy of the man himself.

The game was up. Even the Government couldn't avoid seeing the chaos that resulted from deregulation. Tory 'wet' Chris Patten was installed at the Department of the Environment, and the first step on the road back to reason had been taken.

1988 was also the year of Mrs Thatcher's conversion to the global environmental cause. In her speech to the Royal Society she said: "The Government espouses the concept of sustainable economic development. Stable prosperity can be achieved throughout the world provided the environment is nurtured and safeguarded. Protecting this balance of nature is therefore one of the great challenges of the late twentieth century...". Little did we know that Mr Lawson's tax reforming budget later that year would light the fuse of inflation and cause the deepest recession since the thirties; a recession that, among other things, has also knocked environmental issues down the political agenda.

It is also worth recalling that 1988 was the year when European Community Directive 85/337 on Environmental Impact Assessment came into force in the UK. This challenged the "presumption in favour of development" which the Government had elevated to a fundamental doctrine of planning. For those developments judged to have "significant environmental effects", EIA placed the assumption, in theory, in favour of the environment.

As environmental awareness spread quickly throughout the body politic, thanks largely to brilliant campaigning by militant environmental groups with youthful appeal, Mr Patten ordered the drafting of an unusual White Paper. Published in 1990, it represented a first attempt in the UK to bring the complex web of environmental issues together and set out a detailed programme of action. Since then, the Government (including the Welsh Office) has reported annually on its achievement of the modest goals listed and up-dated in the White Paper.

Less publicly, moves were also afoot at this time to restore the influence of the land-use planning system over development. The Planning and Compensation Bill entered Parliament barely a month after the appearance of the Environment White Paper. Although it was hardly designed to set the world on fire, MPs soon came under skilful lobbying from the Council for Protection of Rural England, and others, who urged them to introduce measures that reflected the thrust of the White Paper. As a result, an uninteresting bill was transformed into one of the most useful pieces of environmental legislation for years.

Many late-night debates in committee caused the Government to rethink its approach. At one stage an amendment that gave important hedgerows legal protection from damage was accepted. This was one of sixty drafted by CPRE. To its embarrassment and shame, the Government called in the whips to get it removed on Third Reading, to calm the fears of its land owning supporters. Four years on, we are still awaiting revised hedgerows legislation — one of the many environmental promises by this Government which remains unfulfilled.

Other important amendments were accepted, however. These included enhanced legal status for the development plan. Section 54a makes it clear that "development control decisions must accord with the development plan unless other material considerations indicate otherwise". Despite the escape route, this places the assumption firmly in favour of the development plan. It has the potential to shift the debate between environment and development priorities from individual planning applications to the content of policies in development plans themselves.

The Government also agreed to recognise Environmental Impact Assessment in primary legislation for the first time, enabling it to use the procedure more flexibly to cover developments, like wind-power stations and ski-slopes, that had slipped through the net. A new legal requirement was also placed on local planning authorities to include policies on the "conservation of natural beauty and amenity" in their development plans in future.

It was, however, the Government's numerous promises to revise planning policy guidance that signalled the beginning of a real shift in attitude and approach. This has resulted in the appearance of a batch of new Planning Policy Guidance Notes (PPGs) and revisions to secondary legislation, since the Bill received Royal Assent in July 1991. Sustainable development has been introduced alongside the requirement to have regard to "environmental considerations" in plan preparation, to undertake an environmental appraisal of alternative development plan options, to give more publicity to planning applications, and to use planning to manage the demand for natural resources such as land, energy, minerals and water.

On the face of it, these changes represent a major step forward in translating international environmental agreements, such as those adopted at the Earth Summit, into objectives for local action. They have increased public expectations of a change in approach, as illustrated in the question put persistently by the Welsh Affairs Select Committee to the Welsh Office during its inquiry into rural housing: What, if anything, has changed in the way planning committees perform their task following the passing of the 1991 Act? The answer the MPs received was not entirely encouraging.

Nonetheless, three key elements in the evolution of planning policy have been noted since the Act. First, sustaining environmental quality is increasingly recognised as the central objective of policy around which other objectives must be tailored to fit. Second, new and more participatory ways of deciding the appropriate scale and location of new development are being advocated. Third, the focus of attention is more on satisfying development needs rather than market demands. In other words, planners are being encouraged to intervene to manage demand, rather than forever trying to meet it.

The question now being asked by environmentalists is whether the planning system can fulfil its environmental promise.[1] A major challenge appears to lie at local level where environmental momentum is being lost as the crunch comes over achieving real changes in the way development is controlled. The fine words of policy guidance are not yet being effectively translated into development decisions that strike a new direction from the past.

Part of the problem seems to lie in the confusion over what "sustainable development" is supposed to mean. In PPG Note 12 the Government makes clear its intention "... to work towards ensuring that development and growth are sustainable. It will continue to develop policies consistent with the concept of sustainable development. The planning system, and the preparation of development plans in particular, can contribute to the objectives of ensuring that development and growth are sustainable".[2]

Some question whether traditional definitions of 'development' and 'growth' are compatible with the concept of environmental sustainability. How can we use finite resources such as land, minerals or fossil fuels in a genuinely sustainable way? How can we sustain projected increases in the demand for energy and fuels from non-renewable sources, or the current production of wastes? Do we have the analytical tools that can help us make the complex and difficult choices that lead towards sustainability? Even if the answer is 'yes', is there sufficient political will to use them?

A large number of definitions of sustainable development are already in circulation. Some observers have drawn distinctions between 'sustainable development', 'sustainable growth', 'sustainable use' and 'sustainable economy'. Most accept that sustainability in its purest form is incapable of being achieved quickly, and in some ways may never be completely realised. Unless natural or deliberately enhanced regeneration matches the use or depletion of a resource, then sustainability is not being met. In some areas of activity we are very far from such a state. A more realistic initial aim might therefore be to reduce unsustainable practices as far as possible.

Although sustainability may not be totally achievable, it is vital that we make substantial progress towards this goal.[3] In so doing, it is crucial the concept does not lose credibility and public support, simply because of expectations that cannot be matched in the real world. Those who advocate sustainability must try to find realistic solutions, and recognise that making tangible progress is as important as the ultimate objective. Indeed, sustainability is better thought of as a process through which the environmental impacts of necessary development are systematically and measurably reduced, rather than some perfect end-state or Nirvana.

In the planning system, the attainment of sustainability does not just require a shift of 'balance' to give more weight to environmental factors, it requires a fundamentally new approach. The balancing of environmental and development interests, which has lain at the heart of the system for so long, has clearly not prevented the continuing and irreversible loss of important environmental resources. Sustainable use of these resources now needs to be the primary objective of planning to ensure that we live within our environmental means and adjust our economic and social objectives accordingly.

The idea of controlling and steering market demands is central to planning. It applies in varying degrees to the way such basic activities as house-building, retailing, industry and quarrying are permitted to develop. However, the usual approach has been to plan land-use to satisfy development demands in the optimal way, economically, socially and environmentally. Thus industrial processes are often allocated land well away from residential areas, new roads usually by-pass established settlements and housing estates tend to be located on the urban fringe, far from the city centre where shops and services have been traditionally located.

Recent planning guidance indicates, however, that the system should be used to limit the consumption of resources, including land, to acceptable levels by "demand management". To achieve demand management in a free market economy to the degree likely to be required is a major challenge. It will be increasingly necessary to distinguish between need and demand. If planning authorities are to succeed in this task they will need to feel confident to refuse planning permission on grounds of lack of need. This will only happen if the Government upholds such decisions on appeal, which is unlikely since it believes developers are the best judge of need.

Several other concepts are emerging as crucial to sustainability. "Carrying capacity" is a term increasingly used to describe the extent to which the environment in any area can tolerate human activity without suffering unacceptable damage. There is scant understanding of what this means in practical terms at present, and a lack of basic data against which changes in environmental quality can be measured. In planning for sustainability, local authorities will have to start by auditing their own environment to establish an accurate picture of its current health and status.

Until such time as carrying capacities have been established with reasonable degree of accuracy, the "precautionary principle" must apply. If there is uncertainty about the environmental effects of a development, and the risks are significant, this argues in favour of a 'do nothing' approach. Social equity is also important, since it is politically risky for one group to impose solutions which condemn others to a lower standard of living, or a degradation in their quality of life. Equity must apply at local, national and international levels, but it is likely to have greatest significance in relation to global agreements to limit the emission of greenhouse gases, since the legitimate aspirations of less developed countries to improve their standard of living will need to be balanced by a substantial cut in consumption in developed countries like Wales.

While sustainability sets its face against unfettered economic growth, since it has usually outstripped the carrying capacity of the environment, it also recognises that degradation is an inevitable consequence of poor housing, endemic unemployment and run-down public services. Clean production systems, combined heat and power centres, zero energy buildings, the capacity to work from home, consumption for need instead of want, are just some of the kinds of development that not only provide work, cultural diversity and intellectual challenge, but also serve to protect and improve the environment.

In guiding this strategy, the planning system must help reduce energy consumption and the production of greenhouse gases such as carbon dioxide. The Government's own research has concluded that land-use planning "could contribute to improved efficiency of energy use in the built environment at all scales".[4] Research from other countries also suggests that appropriate land use policies can have a significant effect on trip generation, distance travelled and energy consumption. In one study, the variation in energy consumption from local transport between two potential patterns of development of an existing settlement was as much as eighty-five per cent.[5] Over half this difference was due to land-use patterns reducing travelling requirements.

Research published jointly by the Departments of the Environment and Transport[6] reaches the following conclusions:

- technological measures aimed at reducing CO_2 emissions from transport "are unlikely to lead to marked reductions in emissions for the foreseeable future";
- the adoption of planning policies to reduce travel demand needs to be co-ordinated with other measures aimed at reducing emissions; and
- planning policies in combination with public transport measures could reduce projected transport emissions by sixteen per cent over a twenty year period.

An inescapable fact is that the Government's own transport policies have the biggest potential to influence the future trend in CO_2 emissions. National Road Traffic Forecasts indicate that, if unconstrained, road traffic will increase by between 69 and 113 per cent by the year 2025. Even the Government's huge road building program cannot accommodate such traffic growth, which will outstrip any conceivable increase in road capacity by an order of magnitude. It is now becoming recognised that road-building generates additional traffic by encouraging car owners to make more frequent and longer trips, and encouraging non-car owners to buy cars. Resistance to this fact by successive Transport ministers stands in sharp contrast to the view of a pre-war incumbent, Leslie Burgen, who acknowledged in 1938 that "The experience of my department is that the construction of a new road tends to result in a great increase in traffic — not only on the new road, but also on the old one which it was built to supersede".

This lesson is being painfully relearned. Former Secretary of State for the Environment, Michael Howard, admitted in October 1992: "Clearly the growth in transport and especially in car use, both actual and forecast, poses a major challenge to environmental policy makers and transport policy makers alike... We must stand back and seek to promote changes in patterns of transport use — both the amount of travel undertaken and the mode people use. Technical fixes are not enough. We need to get back to basics and influence the demand for travel".

The Government has published guidance to local authorities on ways in which certain development policies can minimise private car use. Planning Policy Guidance Note 12 indicates the kind of development that should be encouraged by local planning policies:

- development that makes full and effective use of land within existing urban areas without "town cramming";
- development that is closely related to public transport networks;
- new development that attracts trips (e.g. offices, shops and leisure facilities) located at public transport nodes;
- housing that is located so as to minimise car use for journeys to work, school and other local facilities;
- limitations on town centre car parking;
- appropriate interchanges between public transport networks; and
- positive encouragement of facilities that assist cycling and walking.

Planning policies can also reduce energy consumption outside the transport sector. Closer integration between land use and energy planning could optimise the opportunities for combined heat and power and district heating systems by relating new energy supply infrastructure to existing or proposed development. Similarly, planning policies that influence the form, design, siting, layout and landscaping of buildings can reduce energy consumption by minimising heat loss from building fabric, maximising the access of solar energy and altering the micro-climate.

There are many other ways in which planning can help build a sustainable society. *Planning for Sustainability*, published by the County Planning Officers' Society, explains not only how transport demand and energy consumption can be reduced, but also how the quality of air, water, landscapes, wildlife and the built environment can be protected and enhanced. The Society believes local authorities must gather environmental baseline data against which improvements can be measured.

'Environmental auditing' is in its infancy, however. The aim is to assess the environmental yardsticks such as materials and energy usage, production of waste and impact on wildlife. Objectives are then set for future improvement which are regularly monitored and re-evaluated. In theory it is a powerful management tool because the interaction of all the relevant components of a system are considered at the same time. Land-use policies identified in a development plan can provide an effective way of achieving desirable improvements highlighted by an audit of this kind. The Department of the Environment's guide, *Environmental Appraisal of Development Plans*,[7] offers a systematic method for assessing the environmental impacts of land use planning policies which can then be modified. It can be used at all stages of plan-making but is most effective if applied strategically from the outset. Sadly, support for this method from the Welsh Office seems lukewarm at best, as is so often the case at present with new techniques designed to help deliver sustainability.

The more commonly encountered procedure of Environmental Impact Assessment is usually applied to individual development proposals. EIA got off to a bad start in the UK following the introduction of the European Community Directive. A combination of weak regulations, demanding thresholds before an EIA could be considered, and the lack of useful guidance and quality control has led to widespread scepticism of its value. Add to this the Government's reluctance to extend EIA to plans, policies and programmes (Strategic EIA) and an intense dislike of EU intervention in domestic affairs and it is perhaps surprising that support for EIA has survived at all. That it has is due in part to pressure from environmental groups who have now managed to persuade the Government to make EIA a "policy priority".

Local authorities can do a great deal to extend the application of EIA, especially to their development plans. It can be used to assess the environmental impact of different development plan options. This should become normal practice. At the level of individual development proposals, local authorities should be bolder in asking for further work if an inadequate Environmental Statement is submitted by a developer, and ensure that adequate public consultation is carried out during the assessment process.

Indeed, planning for sustainability should be as much about helping people shape their own environment as it is about providing extra powers and controls. The planning system is well designed to involve people in the development process if it is properly used. It has been fashioned in response to decades of public pressure, such as the campaigns against urban sprawl, suburbanisation and ribbon development in the 1930s and 40s. It must now show itself responsive to the environmental demands of the 1990s and beyond.

A new culture of public involvement is needed. Attitudes as well as procedures need rethinking. It has been argued that members of the public should have the same rights of appeal against local authority decisions as developers do.[8] It is no longer sufficient to use the excuse that because the planning system took away the automatic right of landowners to develop their own land, only they should have the right to appeal if planning permission is refused. This is an anachronism in the 'undeferential 1990s', when everyone should have the right to protect themselves against the damaging environmental effects of development. The public should have a right of appeal when local authorities permit development which conflicts with the policies of their own development plan. In the absence of such a right, the public is being forced to turn to the Local Government Ombudsman to seek redress for perverse planning decisions.

In his 1991 report the new Ombudsman for Wales echoed his predecessor by criticising the extent to which some councils persistently ignore Government planning guidance, the advice of their officers and their own planning policies. He expressed frustration that "...the limited nature of the personal injustice and subsequent remedy, did not adequately reflect the seriousness of maladministration". This is because the Ombudsman system is designed to protect private interests, not commonly held public ones, such as the protection of an attractive, undeveloped countryside.

The public should be able to have decisions to grant permission reviewed in the same way as the appeals system allows developers to have decisions to refuse permission reviewed. Unless carefully designed, however, such a right could encourage every Twm, Dic and Harri and their female equivalents to challenge planning authorities for the most frivolous of reasons. To avoid this, the right should only exist if permitted development materially conflicts with or prejudices the implementation of any of the policies or general proposals of the development plan. The appeal would have to be made by a person who commented on the original application and has good reason to believe the development plan has been ignored. It has been suggested that the Planning Inspectorate could act as an assessor, giving leave for appeal by members of the public in cases which genuinely seem to merit such action.

Despite the current one-sided approach to appeals, the public still has a number of opportunities to influence the planning system at a local level. District councils are now obliged to draw up development plans and both these and county structure plans should address sustainability issues and show how natural beauty and amenity will be conserved.

Plan-making is supposed to involve the public. A 'pre-draft' plan document is usually published to indicate the main issues and objectives identified by planners. Following consultation on this, a 'draft-deposit' plan is published on which comments are invited over a six week period. Planners then try to resolve disagreements between conflicting interest groups by negotiating changes in the wording of policies. Disputes that cannot be resolved are usually heard by an inspector at an Examination-in-

Public or a Public Inquiry at which people who have outstanding objections can speak. The inspector subsequently makes recommendations to the planning authority which may make changes to their plan. Further public hearings can be required before the plan is finally adopted.

There can be problems over the time taken to agree and adopt a plan, but in theory at least, an up-to-date plan is now a powerful tool for directing and controlling development to make it more sustainable. I say "in theory" because we have yet to see how effectively the new plan-based system will work in Wales. This depends on a number of factors. First, the full set of thirty-seven district-wide local plans will need to be finalised. Seven plans were expected by the end of 1993, fifteen in 1994, thirteen in 1995, and three in 1996. One authority may not complete the process until 1997.

Second, it depends on the clarity and thrust of the planning policies contained in these plans. Vaguely drafted policies will prove of little value. They must place care for the environment at the heart of the development process. On both counts the public can use its influence during the consultation phases of plan preparation. Third, it depends how diligently local councillors stick to their agreed policies. Again, public pressure can help. Finally, it depends whether the Secretary of State for Wales backs up councils that abide by their policies, by rejecting spurious appeals from developers, and punishing those councils that regularly ignore their development plans.

All these opportunities to involve people in planning must be used to ensure environmental resources are used sustainably. The system is complex, however, and can be daunting to many. CPRW's local branch committees have a long track record of monitoring the performance of planning authorities. They can use their experience of the system to considerable effect, but even CPRW's volunteers require regular up-dating on policies and procedures. The Campaign runs an annual training programme, which is open to volunteers in other conservation organisations as well. It has published an 'Index of Planning Policies'[9] to enable its branches to identify relevant Welsh Office guidance on subjects that can be used to back up arguments for or against certain types of development. It also recommends CPRE's *Campaigners' Guide to*

Local Plans,[10] for useful hints on how to influence the plan-making process, and *Sense and Sustainability*[11] for a checklist of 'green' planning policies

It is still difficult to have much confidence in the commitment of Welsh Office ministers to sustainability, despite all this guidance. When the former Secretary of State for Wales, David Hunt, published proposals for a Welsh Economic Council, there was scant reference to the environment and absolutely none to the importance of ensuring future development is sustainable. In this respect his ideas mirrored the vision of the Institute of Welsh Affairs whose report, *Wales 2010*, urged a strategy of 4.5 per cent growth per year over the next seventeen years to "put Wales in the top quartile of the most prosperous regions of the European Community by the year 2010".[12]

The report's authors, some of them young executives in companies that might be expected to do well out of the major civil engineering projects that would be required, feel confident that this phenomenal economic growth can be achieved without harming the Welsh environment. But how this beguiling objective is to be achieved without increasing already unsustainable levels of consumption is nowhere spelt out, presumably because the question was never asked. In *Wales 2010*, care for the environment seems to be more about landscaping concrete structures than questioning the need for them in the first place.

A little more encouragement can be drawn from the recent review of strategic planning guidance in Wales. This was carried out for the Secretary of State by county planners, with help from their colleagues in the districts. Their initial consultation document relegated the environment to the final chapter, far behind those on jobs, growth, infrastructure and housing. The only reference to sustainable development was to be found in paragraph 213. Their final report, however, marked a significant shift in thinking: "In developing land-use policies which will take Wales into the 21st Century, the principle of sustainable development has emerged... as the vital issue to be addressed... Strategic Planning Guidance... can provide the framework to begin the necessary work which will have to be undertaken if sustainability is to be given any credence within the development plan system".[13]

Of particular interest was the report's conclusion that Statutory

Green Belts "may be helpful in controlling settlement form". Although not a ringing endorsement, it does hold out hope that urban sprawl, which is becoming a feature of those parts of Wales that are facing the greatest development pressures, will be brought under tighter control. It is widely agreed that Green Belts will only work if they are used in conjunction with a range of other policies that encourage the redevelopment of already urbanised areas, minimise transport demands and enhance the landscape and recreational potential of urban fringe countryside.

Whether Green Belts can be defined on a large enough scale to influence the development impacts of major transport routes like the M4 or the A55, depends on the willingness of the twenty-two new unitary authorities to work co-operatively. Lobbying by CPRW and the County Planning Officers' Society during the passage of the legislation that will bring these authorities into existence on 1st April 1996, forced Welsh Office Ministers, MPs and district planners to confront the threat to strategic planning capacity which could result from the abolition of the current eight counties. Despite ministerial assurances that inter-authority co-operation and collaboration will evolve naturally within the new framework, the past record of county/district and district/district rivalry does not bode well for future strategic thinking or action. The Welsh Office also appears to harbour the illusion that it can fill the gap left by the counties, an idea that will bring a wry smile to the faces of those who know how stretched its planning division already is under the current arrangements.

This illusion is fuelled to a great extent by the current Secretary of State, John Redwood, who appears attracted to the role of 'colonial strategist'. He has spent hours bent over a map of Wales, rather like a Victorian Viceroy of some far-flung Indian state, trying to work out how best to open up its reserves for exploitation by the global economy. Aware too, of the country's great natural beauty and its potential for tourism, he has decided to sweep away the old broad-brush programme of road upgrading with a more strategic approach which places emphasis on three east-west routes — the M4(48), A55 and A465 Heads of the Valleys road.

In so doing, he has pulled off a significant political trick. On the one hand, the Government's clamp-down on public spending made a slowing of the road upgrading programme virtually inevitable. On the other, a fascinating alliance of countryside, environmental and community groups has sprung up in various parts of the country creating political 'hot-spots' around highly sensitive road schemes. By deleting or deferring several of these schemes from his new 'Roads In Wales' programme, Mr Redwood has been able to save money (at least for the time being) whilst also appearing a champion of the countryside and embattled rural communities. Much now rests on the follow-through. How will his new minister of roads, Gwilym Jones, interpret this approach at Pont Padog, or at other sensitive points along the A5, the A40, the A470, the A487 and so on?

Mr Redwood's strategy holds no comfort for those intent on saving the Gwent Levels from a duplicate M4, since their task has become harder. Nonetheless, a spirited response to the Welsh Office's initial public consulation by environmental bodies and local community groups rocked the road-building establishment. A huge majority of those consulted rejected the motorway proposal in principle. Bowed but unbroken, the highway engineers have returned with a modified scheme for further consultation; the aim being, as always, to divide-and-rule.

But there is now real evidence that the public has seen through the 'roads, roads and more roads' programme, even if the Government is still refusing to do so. It is bargaining on the contradiction inherent in public opinion, that while roads are considered 'a bad thing', people will still demand the freedom to use their cars. But a more serious debate is developing in the wake of reports like CPRW's *Wales Needs Transport Not Traffic*[14] focussing on the provision of integrated public/private transport systems. The transport and land use planning system will undoubtedly play a key role in delivering such solutions on the ground, which makes Mr Redwood's decision to rewrite the DoE's progressive Planning Policy Guidance Note 13 on Transport, all the more worrying.

The indirect impacts of roads are also significant. Maintenance and up-grading schemes account for around a quarter of the demand for aggregates — a demand which is set to rise by over sixty percent in Wales over the next fifteen years unless it is brought under control by the Welsh Office. Recent planning guidance shows that ministers are anxious to find new sources of aggregates to meet this demand. They realise, of course, that increased quarrying will cause serious environmental damage and suffering to many communities, so they are trying to export the problems to coastal super-quarries in Scotland and Scandinavia, increase off-shore dredging, and exploit vast quantities of slate waste in Gwynedd. Despite this, quarries in Wales will still have to produce thirty-five per cent more by early next century.

In North Wales, three-quarters of the demand in the region will eventually be met from waste or recycled materials. Attractive though this sounds, vast quantities of slate waste in Gwynedd will be quarried and exported causing severe damage to the landscape, wildlife habitats, the network of rural roads and many Welsh-speaking communities. In South Wales tens of millions of tonnes of crushed rock from coastal super-quarries will have to be landed, probably at Milford Haven where there are deep-water facilities, causing a huge increase in road haulage. The amount dredged from the Bristol Channel will also increase, despite fears that dredging is already affecting beaches, reducing their buffering capacity as sea-level rises due to the greenhouse effect. In Mid Wales new sources of sand, gravel and crushed rock will be needed, not just to meet demand in the region, but that in adjoining areas of England as well. Many areas of beautiful countryside, some protected as special landscapes, could be badly damaged as a result.

Many believe the main threat to the countryside comes from the sheer numbers of people who want to buy a piece of it. The essence of the countryside is that it has a very low level of development, and farming and forestry predominate. If an attempt is made to share it out, only a few will be satisfied, while the vast majority, including many who live there now, will not be able to afford their share, and its special character will be destroyed in the process.

The Government's belief in market forces and what they paraphrase as "personal choice" has led them to conclude that if lots of people want to leave England to live in Wales they should be able to do so. Over the period to 2001 the Welsh Office predicts a population growth of about 80,000 people. Of this total about 40,000 will be migrants from England. The percentage of overall population growth due to inmigration is predicted to be:

1989 - 1991	70%
1991 - 1996	42%
1996 - 2001	48%
2001 - 2006	80%

Most people would be surprised at these figures but might think these migrants are needed to contribute to the success of Welsh industry. However, the great majority will be accommodated in the rural counties of Clwyd, Dyfed and Gwynedd, where planners are being asked to find suitable building plots. This policy of accommodating high immigration rates is likely to be self-fulfilling in that if houses are supplied they will be demanded. It is also highly questionable to base supply on recent high rates of inmigration, given previous low rates in the past. The pressures that large numbers of incomers will place on the countryside, its communities, roads and services, make the environmental and cultural sustainability of this policy highly debatable. Meeting such a lucrative and powerful outside demand could also distract Welsh house-builders from meeting the more important, yet less-profitable needs of the existing population and from securing the provision of genuinely 'affordable housing'.[15]

Planning for sustainability means more than just trying to reduce the consumption of finite resources. It also means trying to encourage and accommodate new, renewable energy technologies, such as wind-power stations. Although the main thrust of policy in planning must be to conserve and maximise the efficiency of the energy produced by conventional means, there should be no mistaking the long term need to increase the production of renewable energy. Wales is particularly well-placed to produce significant quantities of energy from the wind, but there is the real danger that thousands of turbines could transform the uplands of Wales into an industrial landscape.

This would be an appalling prospect, and we should learn to walk before breaking into a headlong charge. If the planning system is sensibly used it can help locate those places where viable quantities of wind energy can be generated without damaging some of the finest landscapes of Wales. While few strategic policies exist to steer wind-power stations to such locations, controversy will continue to rage over individual applications, as developers go for the most visually sensitive, but highest wind energy sites. There is now a serious public backlash against noisy, obtrusive wind-turbines, so it is crucial that wind-farms are planned with care to ensure that they are as environmentally benign as possible.

Little has been said so far about the protection of special areas of landscape and ecological quality. The close connection between land-use planning and the designation of special areas is illustrated by the fact that the 1947 Town and Country Planning Act, which established our Post-War planning system, was swiftly followed by the 1949 National Parks and Access to the Countryside Act. This not only led to the creation of National Parks and Areas of Outstanding Natural Beauty, but Areas (now Sites) of Special Scientific Interest and National Nature Reserves. Important though these and other special areas are as reserves of quality, experience since the 1940s suggests that simply throwing a defensive wall around the best sites without tackling the corrosive effects of man's activities within the wider environment, eventually results in this barrier being breached by a rising tide of environmental degradation.

This has caused bodies like the new Countryside Council for Wales to question the whole post-war approach to site safeguard. Some hearts have missed a beat at the suggestion that defensive forces should be redeployed in a more proactive strategy to change core practices in agriculture, forestry and urban development, for fear that in so doing, defences will be relaxed and those sites which have escaped serious damage could be lost. However, the increasing scale of damage from intensified production systems, pollution, acidification, and major construction projects suggests a radical rethink is probably required. It is entirely consistent with the concept of sustainability that effort should be directed towards changing the nature of development itself. Indeed, there is at last hope that the spiral of degradation can be reversed in some industrial sectors, although protective designations are still likely to be needed for some time.

In this chapter I have tried to show how the capacity of the planning system to monitor the state of the environment, manage the demand for natural resources, and influence and guide development in ways that are more sustainable than in the past, has been greatly enhanced over the last five years. Proper weight should be placed on the development plan, the plan should contain policies on conservation and sustainable development, environmental auditing and assessment techniques should be more widely and rigorously applied, and enhanced opportunities for public involvement in the planning process should be enthusiastically grasped.

But this, on its own, will not deliver sustainability for Wales. Powerful economic and political forces still seem to be pushing in the opposite direction. The feeling that Wales must 'catch up' with materially rich (but environmentally degraded) regions in the UK and Europe, is still prevalent. The future of urban Wales apparently depends on massive infrastructure projects like the Cardiff and Newport barrages, while in rural Wales councillors display open contempt for planning. Yet there can be nothing more unsustainable than a settlement pattern of isolated dwellings, for which access by car is essential. The pain caused by carbon taxes will be all the more difficult to bear in future and irreversible damage will have been done to the countryside, unless the long-term benefits of planning are recognised.

The system, the guidance and the techniques are all there to be used to help move Wales towards sustainability (see Table 1), but this is unlikely to happen unless a political head of steam can be stoked up again on environmental issues. Campaigning environmental groups have a tremendous responsibility to kindle and harness grassroots concern for the future of the Welsh environment. Every battle ground, from the Padog Bends to Carmel Woods, from Cardigan Bay to Crickhowell, must be used to get over the message that future development must be demonstrably sustainable. Such arguments will only carry weight, however, if large numbers of people are galvanised into action in defence of their local environment through the planning system. The opportunities it now offers must be grasped with conviction if we are to create a sustainable Wales.

Notes

1. Burton, T. 'The Planning and Compensation Act — First Annual Report — An Environmentalist's Viewpoint', a paper given to the

joint RTPI/DPOS conference, November 1992.

2. The Welsh Office. 'Development Plans and Strategic Planning Guidance in Wales', Planning Policy Guidance Note 12 (Wales), February 1992.

3. CPRW (1993). 'Wales 2012: The UK National Sustainability Report: Its role and relevance to Wales'.

4. Owens, B and Cope, D. 'Land Use Planning Policy and Climate Change', HMSO, April 1992.

5. Naess, P. 'Urban Concentration Saves Nature', a paper presented to ECE Research Conference in Ankara on Ecological Challenges for Urban Development and Urban Planning, 1992.

6. *Reducing Transport Emissions Through Planning*, HMSO, 1993.

7. Department of the Environment (1993). *Environmental Appraisal of Development Plans*, HMSO, 56pp.

8. CPRW (1993). 'Memorandum of evidence for the Welsh Affairs Committee's inquiry into rural housing', HMSO.

9. CPRW/E (1993). 'Index of National Planning Policies', 23pp.

10. CPRE (1992). *Campaigners' Guide to Local Plans*, 107pp.

11. CPRE (1993). *Sense and Sustainablity*, 48pp.

12. Institute of Welsh Affairs (1993). *Wales 2010*, 139pp.

13. Strategic Planning Forum of the Assembly of Welsh Counties. 'Strategic Planning Guidance in Wales: Topic and Overview Reports', December 1992.

14. CPRW (1994). *Wales Needs Transport Not Traffic*, 40pp.

15. Edwards, J. 'Land of whose fathers', *Rural Wales*, Summer 1993.

Table 1

The kinds of policies that an environmentally-led development plan might include:

- how favoured urban form will be maintained or achieved;
- how the quality of the area's built environment will be conserved;
- how the natural beauty and amenity of the land in the plan area will be protected and enhanced;
- how desired development will integrate with other land uses such as agriculture and forestry;
- how the plan will ensure the efficient use of minerals, water and other natural resources;
- how the plan will minimise the need to travel;
- how a range of opportunities for public enjoyment of open spaces will be provided;
- how recreation and tourism will be accommodated in ways that minimise their environmental impact;
- how the location of employment generating development will be determined within an environmental framework;
- what conditions and benefits will be sought in exchange for planning permission.

Margaret Minhinnick

Winning the Battle, Losing the War? The Future for the Environmental Movement In Wales

In the decade since the miners' strike ended in 1985, and with the temporary exception of the Poll Tax protests, it might be said that the most prominent form of political action to take place in Wales has been motivated by environmental concern. Even language campaigning, and certainly direct action against second homes, have been less well supported than a host of marches, demonstrations, media stunts and lobbying exercises on issues that are essentially environmental in character. These range from energy matters such as radioactive pollution and plans for new nuclear power-stations, the expansion of the opencast coal industry and the development of wind-power, through issues concerning air pollution and toxic waste, to problems of planning and landscape stewardship. (Indeed 'environmentalism', as we shall see, has come to serve as a catch-all definition, somewhat to its detriment, for a huge ragbag of subjects).

What is remarkable about this type of political action is that it has been adopted by many previously politically inactive members of the public, the majority of whom are not obvious supporters of any political party. This activity inevitably runs parallel to the explosion of membership of various environmental bodies in the UK during the last twenty years. For example, in England, Wales and Scotland in 1971, there were approximately 1,000 members of Friends of the Earth. By 1981 that figure in England and Wales had grown to 18,000, and a decade later was a remarkable 112,000. Today in Wales, there are approximately 3,000 members, a highly significant increase on the 600 registered in 1984, but nevertheless a support base which is now in decline. There is also evidence to suggest that the memberships of other Welsh organisations have peaked. (Interestingly, that of Wales' 'leading conservation organisation', the Campaign for the Protection of Rural Wales, never boomed like that of its English equivalent or other such bodies in the 80s. The present figure of 3,500 is roughly the same as it was in 1980. Despite this lack of expansion, the CPRW has succeeded in updating its former fuddy-duddy image [the reason for its stagnation?] and in considerably broadening its profile).

Examination of "the national newspaper of Wales" over the last decade will illustrate that issues such as acid rain, the importation of toxic substances, marine pollution and waste recycling have received a very wide and often repetitive coverage. Television and radio have also played vital roles in bringing matters of the environment to almost the entire Welsh population. Various fundamental conclusions may be gleaned from this decade of high media profile and intense activity on environmental matters.

The first is that the Welsh population is now far better informed on subjects of environmental priority than it was a decade ago. However, as environmental issues become more technical and specialised, there is an increasing danger that professional environmentalists will find themselves too far removed from the wellsprings of popular interest and support to be able to use effectively, or to comprehend the nature of, public concern.

The second is that none of the political parties in Wales have understood or been able to harness the massive surge in political energy which has been released by environmental campaigning. Bewildered by the specificity, the difficulty and at times the sheer size of the issues tackled by pressure groups, action networks and committed individuals, the four main Welsh parties have simply had no idea of how to work with the new environmentalism, or ensure themselves of its vote. The male traditionalists of Welsh politics have proved themselves as uncomfortable with this new dynamism as a group of middle-aged fathers waiting to pick up their teenage daughters after a dance. Seen by some politicians as an embarrassing indictment of their own political work, and by others as an alien manifestation in Wales, further proof of the creeping anglicisation of the culture, no Welsh political party can claim to have either understood or supported the explosion of environmentalism.

The third is that the environmentalists themselves have failed to change significantly the way that politics are run in Wales, or how and where political power over environmental quality and protection is exercised. What real achievements there have been — the election of Cynog Dafis to Westminster under the Plaid/Green ticket in 1992, and the eleven per cent of the vote captured by the Welsh Green Party in the 1989 European elections — cannot compare with the victories won and progress made by language campaigners. These include the establishment of the S4C television channel, the increasing provision of education in the Welsh language, and smaller, but importantly visible achievements such as bilingual roadsigns and government and private utility documents. This is clear evidence, to those who need it, of an increasing degree of official status and of burgeoning linguistic morale.

Somewhat ironically, because of their media profile, the environmentalists have much less to show, both in terms of support from the political establishments of Wales, and in lasting campaign successes. Of course, this is partly due to the fact that politics in the UK has developed in a vertical, not horizontal, manner. The various ministries and departments stand like tall, isolated pillars, between which there is very little linkage or means of communication. Because of this system, even the belief that environmental protection and understanding will be achieved by the 'trickle down' method, trumpeted by the most ardent centralists and paternalists, is obviously flawed.

The lack of success has also a good deal to do with the nature of the issues tackled. Seasoned campaigners know that "victories" in halting opencast expansion or unnecessary by-passes are often only mere postponements of threats. Also, the green dreams of the 70s and early 80s, if fulfilled in the 90s, can possess a decidedly bittersweet quality. For example, the targeting of upland Wales by commercial wind-farm developers, once a remote and attractive campaign goal for many, has proved the source of splits and deep unhappiness in the environmental movement. The refusal of the nuclear industry to lie down and die throws into doubt the permanence of the success in halting Wylfa 'B', whilst it can be argued that it was not simply pressure from protesters that succeeded in shutting down the Magnox reactors at Trawsfynydd but the fact that, like an old car, the nuclear plant had already been run into the ground.

Moreover, for urban environmentalists, the current crass 'American strip culture' development of the outskirts of Cardiff, Swansea, Bridgend and other towns, is a nightmare come true. The 'McDonalds-McJobs-McLives-McWorld'-style existence, satirized and mournfully chronicled by American novelist Douglas Coupland, has jumped out of the pages of his book *Generation X* (a text all environmentalists should read) and into the green fields of the Vale of Glamorgan and Clwyd.

It is therefore important to seek answers to two questions. The first is why environmentalists have not achieved more in Wales. The second is how to identify the future areas into which today's environmentalism should attempt to expand. The answers to the first question are simple. The greens — and here I mean the plethora of one subject action groups — are under-achievers because most campaigners insist on looking only at their own backyards and are unwilling or unable to link issues, or network meaningfully with other groups. Also, some major matters such as opencast coal expansion, occur in places which are either politically debilitated or where people have other urgent priorities. (Often, these are health related. A June 1994 report from the Census Office indicates that 21.5 per cent of the Welsh population is incapacitated in some form by 'chronic' or long-term illness. This is the worst record of all four 'home countries', and certainly the percentage will be far higher in opencast coalfield areas.) On top of this, a campaign can possess the wrong 'image'. Despite continuous protests against opencasting and exhaustive media coverage of this issue, it seems almost impossible to encourage the participation of young people.

Other reasons for under-achievement include the fact that organisations like Friends of the Earth in Gwynedd and Dyfed are largely (with some honourable exceptions) comprised of English incomers, most of whom have not learned Welsh. For example, the

National Committee of Friends of the Earth Cymru currently comprises ten individuals, seven of whom were born outside Wales — an astonishing figure for a 'Welsh' organisation. Other bodies, such as the Campaign for the Protection of Rural Wales, the RSPB. and the Wildlife Trusts are often perceived as middle-aged and middle-class, whilst Greenpeace has no Welsh base or roots.

Moreover, these organisations, usually staffed by keenly political people with more than the environment on their minds, exist in states of fractious exhaustion, a result of their incessantly reactive, green fire-brigade role. Other groupings, such as The Ramblers, the National Trust and the Civic Trust attract hobbyists, specialists and people not interested in exploring the possible political influence and role of their organisations.

Nevertheless, all of the bodies mentioned above, the combined memberships of which, totalling almost 85,000 in 1994, should make them more influential than they actually appear, today find themselves in stages of significant change. The differences between them are starting to blur, a process encouraged by the government-funded initiative, 'Environment Wales', the creation of the 'Wales Countryside and Wildlife Link' coalition, and hastened by changing policy styles and public attitudes.

For example, at the beginning of the last decade, Friends of the Earth was at the start of its expansion in Wales, and possessed a (false) reputation for extremism. Today it boasts twenty-five, admittedly small, local groups, and is easily the most visible component of the Welsh green movement. In England, Friends of the Earth and Greenpeace are bastions of the 'alternative establishment', bodies that have succeeded in largely rewriting the environmental agenda in the UK — an immense achievement. Yet in the process, Friends of the Earth in particular has lost its 'sharp end' status as other organisations have radicalised their messages. Today, it is an assemblage of what Americans term "banner-hangers", researchers and letter-writers, worthy, influential and a little tired, its members unsure whether to feel proud or resentful as they see 'their' issues and opinions adopted by other pressure-groups.

It seems likely that in this decade the differences between what were the opposite poles of the green movement — the so-called 'extreme', as exemplified by Friends of the Earth, and the conservative, in the shape of the Council for the Protection of Rural England and the Campaign for the Protection of Rural Wales — will diminish as the former becomes an essentially research, publication and information technology-entrenched organisation and the others toughen their images. Such developments might be inevitable (if only for the sake of coherence and the pooling of strengths) for it seems certain that politics and the public will continue to admit the general urgency of the environmental situation, even if significant legislative and lifestyle changes have yet to match our media-inspired green awareness.

However, this will lead to disaffection of the more radical activists. Indeed, what might now be required in Wales is the emergence of a new, street-level organisation, backed by computer technology, such as a native, bilingual 'Earth First!', if only to energise an increasingly polite and middle-aged environmental scene. Dangerously, there is already present in this country an unhealthy divide between 'professional' organisations and the significant reservoir of well-informed, often angry activists, many of them self-employed or 'unemployed' in the old sense, and having time and skills to devote to causes of their choice.

In the US there exists a wide variety of groups, with names like 'Lifeweb', 'Keep it Wild' and 'Redwood Action Team', all aligned to 'Earth First!' because of that organisation's youthful and energetic vision of how political action can be defined. We can expect to see short-lived, one issue groups such as this springing up in Wales, impelled by visions of environmental apocalypse, influenced more by American authors such as Jerry Mander, Robert D. Kaplan and the 'monkey-wrenching' stories in the Earth First! newspaper than Jonathon Porritt or David Bellamy, and inspired in part by the campaign tactics of *Cymdeithas yr Iaith*.

(However, it needs stating here that in the USA at least, certain sections of Earth First! are already displaying a worrying 'anti-people' characteristic in their environmentalism. Calls for an immediate halt to industrial development and economic expansion are made with no understanding of the effects such social cataclysms would cause for ordinary workers. Earth First! in fact should learn that politics cannot be practised if people are not the most important part of the equation. Its activists need to conclude that for real environmental progress, they must begin to love the trapper as well as the grizzly bear. And that is a necessary lesson for all of us.)

With the proliferation of desktop publishing and information technology, and the increasing knowledge and confidence of home-based activists, the 'professional' green organisations might well be by-passed in the future, especially if their staff are compelled by their new respectability to devote their time to writing responses to government discussion papers and important, but invisible, lobbying. Like everything else, radicalism has its cycles. Computers and easier access to environmental data could well invalidate the existence of centralised, professionally-run offices, with their 'management-staff-volunteer' hegemonies. Indeed, it could be argued that the only thing that will maintain the discrete existence of the current crop of environmental organisations is their appetite for image-branding in the media, and the perpetuation of their individual names. This is already a major cause of dissatisfaction felt by Wales' growing number of unaligned, self-funding activists.

But it would be fatal to see computer and information technology as the key to a green future. In a small country like Wales, more influential good for the environment can still be achieved by a meeting over a drink or a sympathetic phone call. Here, individuals count. How many Welsh politicians spend any significant time in front of an Apple Mac, for instance? Computers are great levellers in the sense that they allow us all a similar degree of mediocrity, an equal ability to be colourless or aloof. (I write this in the knowledge that the Internet or "Information Superhighway" is already, inescapably, with us.) Crucially, computers are also tools which will enable the affluent to construct even deeper bunkers for themselves and arrange for greater insulation against environmental problems. They are amongst the weapons that will help ensure that what have been termed 'environmental privileges' — clean air, unpolluted water — will continue in certain parts of the world to be available only to the few.

The answers to the second question — in what areas of concern do environmentalists now need to display an informed and practical interest if they are to achieve political change and attract public support — are much more difficult to answer. Of course the perennial, not to say predictable and sometimes (to be frank) desperately tedious, problems of acidification, marine pollution and waste management will remain with us. But it also appears clear that the environmental issues of the near future will require skills and enthusiasms different from those most often demonstrated today by activists.

What is vital for Wales is that landscape campaigners — those who seek to protect hillsides from wind-farms and woodlands from quarries, and to whom the topography is precious, even sacred — broaden their aims. This would first mean accepting that much of Wales is now threatened, not by the work ethic, as in the past, but by the leisure principle. Coal, for example, destroyed one environment and created another, obliterated a rural culture and nurtured an urban lifestyle that itself has now fragmented. Today, affluence and free time, linked with private transport, ensure that tourism is our most economically important and also our most invasive industry. Tourism is a curious phenomenon. It undermines a culture whilst seeming to support it, disfigures a future whilst appearing, at least, to guarantee one.

Thus we need to beware of both sentimentality and paganistic flummery as we look at the landscape of Wales. When we acknowledge the grandeur or the beauty of a scene we should also note that it is our economic circumstances that primarily afford us the time and the opportunity for such detailed appreciation — circumstances that have in all likelihood come about by destructive environmental practices elsewhere. We should also concur that an aesthetic attachment to a landscape as a main campaigning impulsion might not be enough to preserve it in an age when the threats to the cultures and habitats that that landscape sustains are increasingly insidious.

Thus those who oppose wind-farms must also devote equal time to how we can achieve a coherent energy policy with the least possible destructive impact; those who work to prevent quarrying in Dyfed or Gwynedd should also consider how employment might be provided to ensure that local Welsh (and English) speakers are not compelled to desert their own communities to search for work; and that everyone who campaigns to preserve the 'beauty' or 'wildness' of Wales acknowledges that the success of their efforts could well increase the tourist pressure on this country, thereby ensuring that those qualities are less frequently identifiable or are compromised by other means.

This concept of 'the leisure ethic' is an important one for Wales. The country is now more aggressively marketed than ever before as well worthy of any visitor's time. Tom Jones and Anthony Hopkins stare down from advertising hoardings that claim it is the quality and variety of its environment that make Wales the discerning tourist's choice. To certain people tourism is manna from Heaven; to others it is more destructive than acid rain. (Some go further than this. The French, for example, have described the arrival and dissemination of EuroDisney culture in the Isle de France as a 'cultural Chernobyl', despite the fact that many jobs have been created by the initiative.) In Orange County, Florida, a staggering eighty per cent of employment is created by tourism, and recently (I write in June 1994) a midnight curfew on local people was introduced because of criminal assaults on visitors. The obvious response is that tourism has become such a monstrous 'success', at least in Orange County, that it now not only interferes with culture and the environment but also basic human rights. But whatever the perception of tourism, environmentalists seeking direction as to where they might usefully direct their time and energies can no more ignore it than they can questions of public and private transport or electricity generation.

Perhaps an even greater imperative for the environmental movement is that it now seeks to display far better understanding and keener sympathies towards the existing cultures of Wales. This means working jointly with others to maintain linguistic and community values, whether in the valleys of Gwent or the villages of Snowdonia. (In this respect it is good to see the adoption of the former Director of the CPRW to a position on the Welsh Language Board.) One reason for the political negligence of green issues in Wales is that it has been perceived by many that despite widespread sympathy for environmentalism, the environmentalists themselves possessed little grassroots backing or popularity.

Giving support to the culture by protecting the environment might best be achieved by our environmental organisations if they worked more closely with bodies that are generally described as the 'caring sector', and which deal with the young, the old, the disabled, the disadvantaged, the homeless and the threatened.

74

Networking with pensioners' organisations on fuel taxation and energy conservation, could for example, help to allay the impression that environmentalists are fonder of other species and their habitats than the human.

Similarly, co-operating with the key radical pressure groups such as *Cymdeithas yr Iaith* could create alliances which would influence the mainstream parties. Such new policies would assist in dispelling the notion that green campaigners 'talk down' to the public and betray the characteristics of the 'do as I say not as I do' school of behaviour. Also crucial in Wales is the development of a far stronger urban environmentalism than exists at present. There is no romance in campaigning for improvements to the shocking statistic that one in thirteen homes in Wales is deemed unfit for human habitation. However, there is much political credibility and support from currently uninterested sectors of the population to be won.

Of equal importance to identifying to a far greater degree with the agencies of cultural and social support, is the need for the Welsh environmental movement to examine its primarily reactive, knee-jerk manner of working — especially at times of sudden threat. It is best here to use a medical analogy. When I instigated the creation of Friends of the Earth Cymru in 1984, the issues the organisation took on made it seem that we were treating three or four inflamed spots on the body of an obviously sick patient. At the height of our work — around 1992 —we were dealing with approximately twenty of those spots. However, whether or not an ulcer vanished, the patient remained unwell. The answer to this appears simple but requires a change of philosophy together with a shift in practice to ensure it works.

The environmental movement, which has built up loyal memberships, a variety of skills and access to modest funding, must move away from the simply prescriptive or diagnostic style in which it now works to a new, preventative emphasis. In my time as the co-ordinator of a green Welsh organisation, I spoke to literally thousands of people who had rung my office to complain about a pollution incident or act of destruction *that had already occurred*. Needless to say, I became adept at helping those people close a series of stable doors.

Equally frustrating was what I describe as the narrowing and deepening of environmentalism. This has occurred as 'issues' have not only multiplied but obviously now require considerable specialist study to comprehend their real gravity. Such issues include at various times the scares about the growth of toxic blue algae on waterways, the presence of 'toxic fish' in our rivers, migration of toxins from packaging into food, the technology required to sterilise sewage with ultra-violet light, and so on. All these and other 'issues' are highly important. Yet compared with continuing ruinous unemployment, the dreadful legacy of poor health in Wales exacerbated by bad diet, drinking, smoking, and air pollution, the neglected condition of many schools, the fact that in one Welsh county over thirty per cent of pupils depart the education system every year without any qualifications, they seem banal and a cul-de-sac for political concern. Environmentalists must realise that these 'bread and butter' matters, which seemingly belong outside the remit of the green groups, have far more serious and long term environmental consequences than certain of the problems we have taken to our hearts and which now consume our time.

Groups like Greenpeace have been brave and ambitious enough to adopt 'issues' such as waste incineration, chlorine pollution and ozone destruction which have required detailed and long research. Friends of the Earth possesses activists who work entirely on "water and toxics" or "recycling" or "roads". The result has been a replication of the problems with Government mentioned earlier. Instead of creating a wide base of understanding, a series of vertical campaign edifices has been erected, which not only fail to communicate with one another, but actually compete for publicity via television and radio interviews and column inches in newspapers — the barometers chosen to measure the success or otherwise of pressure groups.

Personally, if I could choose a way forward, and with the hard won knowledge that no matter how frequently or swiftly an environmental group reacts to a problem, it is never frequent or swift enough, I would merge all such campaign departments into one which researched how sustainable local employment could be created that worked with, and not against, the environment and the requirements for good human health.

The final new area that I should recommend the environmental movement to concern itself with is that of local democracy. This would involve developing a clear opinion on greater independence for Wales itself and how local government within the country should function. Two views are most often expressed. The first is that Wales is a geographically, historically and culturally defined whole which will only ensure environmental protection for itself when far greater political powers are devolved from London to Cardiff and then out to the regions.

The other is that the concept of the 'state' is merely a recent invention of the West, and has proved a disaster in Africa, where national boundaries have been drawn that do not match ethnic divisions, and a means of repression in the former communist bloc. Those who propound this view claim that until the present century, only three per cent of the world's land surface was subject to 'statehood'. They also point out that Wales has never existed as one independent, cohesive entity, and that the real boundaries of states are drawn by modern economics, not history. They further argue that typical 'Welsh' environmental problems such as open-casting, oil and gas exploration, and air and marine pollution, are often the result of political decisions and bad practices beyond our boundaries and control. Of course, all of the above can be used as arguments for the continued political suffocation of Wales within a 'British state'.

The debate is unremitting, but whatever the opinion of environmentalists, they should seriously consider the idea of entering local politics and actually joining a political party. The idea that the explosion of green consciousness in the late 80s would bring into existence a politically powerful rainbow coalition of pressure groups which would replace the traditional parties is dead. Demonstrating on the margins of society has its importance, but I would urge the activists to consider the possibility of eventually sacrificing their (self-estimated) ideological purity for practicality. Constant lobbying of those in power, combined with the belief that you could do a better job than the power-holders, yet simultaneously refusing to step into the grimy arena of local politics, is not a position that grown-ups should wish to hold for too long. My belief is that if a fraction of those people who had enthusiastically joined green organisations in the 80s had also ventured into their communities' political parties, then environmentalism would now be far better established as a basic political principle.

This brings us to the question of the Green Party as a suitable vehicle for environmental activism. Regretfully, I would advise those people with energy and time who want to become active in an environmental/political sense to choose instead one of the four established Welsh 'grey' parties.

The failure of the greens to capitalise on their marvellous showing in the 1989 European elections (fifteen per cent of the English vote, eleven per cent in Wales, declining to four per cent and under three per cent respectively in June 1994) has occurred because the party was not able to turn its ideals into practical policy alternatives, its energies into achievements, its enthusiams into ideas that ordinary people can understand. Instead, it has been guilty of perpetuating a level of internal strife that makes Labour and the Conservatives look like happy families. Fatally, it has also tried to imitate the pressure groups, placing far too much emphasis on global, 'no-win' issues like ozone destruction, when such matters are already more expertly covered by Greenpeace and Friends of the Earth. It is equally at fault for devoting too little time to questions of employment and education. Unfortunately, it has also been guilty — like most in the environmental movement — of a 'holier (or greener) than thou'-type hubris which resulted in its electoral come-uppance in the 1994 European election.

As far as the Welsh Green Party goes, this is little short of tragedy, because its activists are amongst the most articulate in Wales. Nevertheless, the party as a whole has failed to realise that politics is a sordid business of compromise and trade-offs. Describing the other national parties as 'grey' implies that the people who vote for them are also of that hue. There will be no sudden sea change in our politics. The new orthodoxy is that we must be patient until (early in the next century?) a new generation of politicians has taken over in the parishes, Cardiff and Westminster, a generation brought up in an age when the last residual resentment for the continued exuberance of the Welsh language has vanished, together with the remaining hostility towards 'environmentalism'. Before such a generation appears, we will lose further precious sites, endure more gross pollution, waste more irreplaceable resources. But we will also work towards real achievements.

One point that needs to be made strongly here is that Welsh environmentalism has been impelled as much by women as by men. Welsh Friends of the Earth groups, for instance, often show a heavy majority of women members. (Indeed environmentalism is itself often very different between the sexes. Women are the instinctive greens, and from an early age might comprehend the principles of sustainable lifestyles, even if unable to live by them. Men take on issues, often very fiercely, in a similar way as they become supporters of football teams. Male environmentalists collect and quote statistics as ardently as trainspotters seek rare coach numbers.) Such integral female participation is the opposite of what can still occur in Welsh political parties, dominated as they are by a power-broking male gerontocracy, the existence of which deters many women from even considering party political involvement.

Where I believe Welsh environmentalists will not venture, is into the quagmire-like business of population growth. At least, our contribution will not occur in a primitive, head-counting fashion. It remains necessary, however, for activists to adapt their current global perspectives. Until recently, these have been manifested as concern for the fate of rainforest peoples in South America and South East Asia. Indeed, it is said of Welsh greens that they are more sympathetic to the cultures and livelihoods of rainforest tribes than to either the survival of the Welsh language or the working classes of the Valleys and Clwyd who would never dream of joining Friends of the Earth or the Civic Trust.

Protection for the rainforests and their inhabitants is vital. But I would hope to see our environmental movement taking an equal interest in the lives of the urban poor, who constitute a major percentage of the world's population. Such people are not 'ecologically tuned in' to their 'natural' environment as the rainforest dwellers are, although they have heroically, and appallingly, adapted to the conditions into which they are born. These anonymous, unchronicled tribes survive in sewers, shanties and rubbish tips. They steal, beg, deal in drugs and prostitute themselves and each other. They frighten and embarrass the affluent. They are detrimental to a city's tourist image. Because of this, in places like Rio de Janeiro, they are rounded up and murdered. On many streets in that city it is easy to step from an environment of wealth and privilege, where the whole world seems divinely ordered to maintain the fortunate few in conditions of luxury and ease, into a parallel universe which has already been utterly degraded and its inhabitants brutalised. Yet the urban poor have as much to teach us about our planet as the native horticulturists and pharmacists of the forests. Welsh environmentalists have a modest role in listening to their lessons.

The title of this essay, I believe, betrays the realism and not the cynicism of its author. In the last decade enormous advances have been made in the popular perception of environmental issues, and for this we can thank a host of energetic, motivated people. However, the euphoria of the late 80s — when some of us actually believed we were going to change the world — has evolved into a grim acceptance that the severity and the complexity of the problems we face are far deeper than we imagined.

For example, the environmental movement's greatest educational ally has been television. But we are now increasingly aware of the type of pollution that the media themselves are responsible for, and the effects this has on culture, self-image and political activity. This is far worse than Bruce Springsteen's line about there being "forty-seven channels and nothing on" suggests. Media pollution includes the tabloidization of values, the reduction of 'lifestyle' to an orgy of consumerism, and the definition of 'freedom' simply as the ability to exercise product choice. It is vital that environmentalists address it.

Finally, there are three practical projects to which all Welsh environmentalists should offer support, and which can act as unifying factors in our work.

First, we should welcome the CPRW's idea that a 'Centre for Sustainability' be created in Wales, to profile and encourage the best environmental practices in planning, design, construction, impact and influence. (Such a Centre should have been the lasting legacy of 1992's Wales Garden Festival, one of our great missed opportunities.)

The second is the resourcing of a Wales Energy Council which would determine the energy requirements of this country for the next several decades and construct policies on how that energy might be created, using minimum environmental and cultural impacts as its criteria. The concept of a self-sufficient and self-sustaining Wales in terms of energy generation and use should be debated as decisively as possible. One of the first aims of the council would be to produce a costed programme for complete lagging, insulation and part-provision of energy efficient lighting, for every home in Wales.

The third is that the existing Centre for Alternative Technology, near Machynlleth, a world-class establishment of its kind, and a highly important tourist destination (even if not served by good public transport) should receive significant state support and be allowed to expand and market itself globally. Perhaps only in this way will that present emphasis on 'alternative' (unfortunate, hippie-era word) be swept away to be replaced by 'sustainable'.

These projects may not change the world but they certainly belong at the forefront of our agenda. By supporting them and the cultural and social issues referred to earlier, the Welsh environmental movement might prove that it now combines fervent idealism with a degree of political maturity. It would also indicate that we have broken out of the 'green ghetto' in which we consistently preach to the converted, compete with allies for money and members, and delude ourselves with the notion that our principles and activities allow us the occupation of moral high ground denied to those who as yet do not share our concerns.

John Barnie

The Suburban Park — Conservation, Tourism and Decay

Population pressure is the main cause of environmental damage in Wales although this is far from evident to many of us who live here. After all, it can be argued, over-population and consequent degradation of nature are notoriously Third World problems. Wales is an industrialised nation and haven't many of the industrialised nations managed to stabilise their populations, reversing the upward demographic trend of nearly two centuries?

Statistics might seem to bear this out. Depending on which model is used, world population is estimated to rise from its present 5.5 billion to 10 and perhaps 12.5 billion by the middle of the twenty-first century. Ninety-seven per cent of this increase is expected to take place in the Third World. It is the horrific Malthusian implication of these figures which caused Henry Kendall of the Union of Concerned Scientists to comment recently that: "Population control is a co-determinant with control of environmental damage. People who take issue with control of population do not understand that if it is not done in a graceful way, nature will do it in a brutal fashion".

Images come easily to mind of domestic herds eating every leaf and thorn in the sub-Saharan scrub land, or of pleated, eroded hills in Madagascar, denuded of forest by the desperate need to farm. It's hard to believe that this is an immediate problem for Wales.

However, the ninety-seven per cent growth projection for the Third World is only part of the population crisis, as another statistic shows. At present, the industrialised nations constitute no more than twenty-five per cent of the world population, a percentage which will decline still further in the next fifty years. Currently, however, we consume seventy-five per cent of energy used, according to the US. Environmental Defence Fund.[1] This means that the average nuclear family in New York, London or Bonn (to use an often-quoted example) consumes as much energy in a year as an entire village in Bangladesh.

In terms of the stress we place on the Earth's energy resources, the industrialised nations are proportionally as over-populated as many parts of the Third World. For this reason alone we are deeply implicated in localised and global environmental damage and if radical changes are not implemented now, we will suffer its consequences just as surely as people in the Third World, if more slowly and by different pathways.

*

High energy consumption is a necessary consequence of our market-led machine culture. It takes large amounts of energy to produce the machines and other goods we are persuaded to need, and large amounts of energy for the constant servicing and extension of the culture's material superstructure. The environmental damage caused by this, including the acidification of much of Wales' upland moors, is well-known.

Equally significant is what might be termed the secondary consumption of energy by the individual as he and she try to act out the dream life of leisure and mobility predicted by machine culture. This is also damaging to the environment but is much less easy to come at because of a fundamental trait in human psychology — our inherent self-regard. We find it comparatively easy to express concern over pollution which can be blamed on society as a whole — SO_2 emissions from coal-fired power stations, for example, in which the individual's responsibility can be muddied over and blamed on the system. For the system must then find a solution, absolving the individual in the process.

What are not easy to acknowledge are the specifics of personal involvement. When pressed, the individual soon becomes enmeshed in special pleading and rationalisation, justifying the need for a car, a foreign holiday and a hundred other things, in terms which attempt to separate out his or her particular acts from general social trends. When argued for in this way, car ownership becomes a badge of individual freedom; only when cars are thought of collectively in their millions does it become impossible to evade the machines' (and their owners') involvement in large-scale environmental damage.

For it is one of the ironies of machine culture that the promise it holds out is in the end illusory and must be so for purely mathematical reasons. Mobility and extended leisure may in themselves be good, they may even be fundamental rights in a democratic society, but when pursued without limit by millions in a finite geographical space, they rapidly destroy the foundations of the freedom and individual self-expression they are meant to reflect. This is the predicament we find ourselves in now. It is a predicament Wales shares of course with all the industrialised nations, which is why a solution, if there is one, cannot be arrived at in isolation.

*

Since the 1960s increased mobility due to the growth of car ownership has had a number of effects, all of which seemed positive at first. Families had greater choice as to where they lived and worked. It became possible to commute fifteen, twenty, thirty miles from the country to the town. Leisure activities were no longer limited more or less to the immediate locality but could be pursued further and further from home, a development which in turn created demand for a greater variety of such activities, leading to the rapid creation of a profitable leisure 'industry'. The nuclear family commuting to work and school in two or three directions from a converted cottage or farm or a new estate, spending its weekends yachting, pony trekking, scuba diving, rally driving, picnicking, happy and smiling, is an image implanted in our minds from a thousand advertisements. It may not be what we have at the moment, but it's what the culture persuades us to want and strive for. And it's an alluring image, not to be discarded lightly by those for whom it is a goal or by those who have it in their grasp. We tend therefore to ignore or play down the material life's increasingly negative effects, or to look for alternatives that will mitigate the damage and allow us to live on in machine culture's dream.

But in Wales especially we cannot afford this because the changes in work and domicile patterns produced by increased mobility are taking place on a scale that threatens to overwhelm us as a nation. The reason of course is that these changes are not simply occurring *within* Wales, but on a much larger scale *between* Wales and England.

England itself is in a state of material and cultural decline (the legacy of its early ruthless industrialisation and the creation and loss of Empire) which is unlikely to be reversed in the foreseeable future. But there are sufficient numbers amongst its millions who are aware of this and have the financial resources to do something about it in personal terms by getting out. For such people Wales is an attractive alternative. Not only are large areas of countryside here still relatively unspoilt, remote communities are all the while being brought within reach of Liverpool, the Midlands, Bristol and London, as east-west road connections are improved.

According to a report published by Mintel, *Regional Lifestyles 1992*, at least 13 million people want to move from Britain's decaying cities and up to 4 million plan to do so within five years, with rural Wales as one favoured area of resettlement.[2] No doubt many who expressed this intention were indulging in wishful thinking, but the report confirms a demographic shift which has been under way for some fifteen years and which has already had profound consequences for rural areas close to the English conurbations, from East Anglia to Wales.

Some of the consequences as far as Wales is concerned can now be given a statistical framework as results of the 1991 Census begin to be released. It is clear, for example, that certain areas have effectively become English enclaves as a result of inmigration. Radnor is possibly the most dramatic example. Its population grew rapidly in the decade since the 1981 Census, but that growth was entirely due to inmigration. In 1981 thirty-nine per cent of the district's population was born in England; that percentage had risen to forty-six per cent by 1991. During the decade the number of residents born in England rose by 2,700 while the number born in Wales declined by c.170. Similar trends are revealed for other favoured areas such as the Clwyd coastline and Monmouth in Gwent.[3]

The social and environmental cost of this rapid demographic shift is suggested in a survey of the parish of Norton conducted by the Radnor branch of the Campaign for the Protection of Rural Wales.[4] At the time of the 1961 Census the parish population was 174. This had jumped to around 400 by 1990, an increase of 130 per cent in thirty years. During this period there was no significant growth in the farming community. Growth was due almost entirely to the inmigration of elderly people who had retired to the countryside and mature people who had moved to Norton with a view to retirement. Of the latter, several commuted to work as far afield as the Midlands and London. A large percentage of those questioned for the survey said they had moved to Norton "to live in a beautiful countryside and to enjoy the tranquillity and pleasantness of village life".

These stated reasons are the expected ones, revealing the inmigrants of Norton as close kin to the tourists. It would be nice to be culturally and socially invisible, insinuating one's way into a community to enjoy its benefits without disrupting its fabric. And that can even happen to an extent, when demographic change is slow. Then incomers can both enrich a host community and be slowly absorbed by it in one or two generations.

But when the pace of demographic change is swift and the numbers involved are large, the host community cannot be sustained, it fragments to become part of a different kind of social grouping, an agglomerate of individuals and nuclear families without cohesion and dominated by outsiders.

Naturally it is possible to create new communities out of short-term demographic upheaval, as happened in the South Wales valleys during the process of industrialisation in the early nineteenth century. But there initial large-scale population shifts were followed by periods of comparative stability and integration. This is not happening today. Norton is fast becoming a retirement village in which population loss through death amongst the old is made up by a steady influx of retirees to create a perpetual 'community' of strangers.

This is not the only pattern of inmigration into Wales, of course. Elsewhere, in Dyfed and Gwynedd for example, many inmigrants are young nuclear families. This does not necessarily create the conditions of stability essential to community formation, however.

The uprootedness of so many rural populations today is a function of society's mobility and a commitment to life-style rather than place. Familial and friendship networks are likely to be spread across Britain and beyond. Values are eclectic and media- and consumer-based. Under these conditions the young leave home easily in pursuit of education, employment and new horizons, for they have no rootedness of kinship in community, and are no more committed to one place than to another.

*

One material consequence of rapid population increase in rural areas is speculative building, the only purpose of which is profit. When this happens, gradual development to meet local needs is subsumed in the hurried building of uniform estates that surround and eventually engulf a village, field by field. Rates of house-building in Norton village are instructive. According to the CPRW report, only nineteen per cent were built prior to 1945. Twenty-three per cent were built between 1945 and 1970, and a massive fifty-eight per cent in the twenty years between 1970 and 1990. In-filling accounts for a small percentage of the increase, but most is due to the building of four estates — one council estate and three private. (Not included in the percentage figures above is a permanent caravan site built in the 1970s with 40 caravans housing retirees mostly from outside the village.) There is currently planning permission for another estate of approximately thirty-five houses.

Given its location in attractive countryside within reach of English conurbations, Norton can consider itself lucky to have escaped so lightly — even though development has utterly changed the social structure of the village. It is, however, a microcosm of what is happening all over rural Wales and indeed Britain. For what we are witnessing is the relentless urbanisation of the countryside, as the demographic drift from cities and speculative property development reinforce each other.

And urbanisation doesn't stop at house building, of course. Rapid growth of villages and towns leads to an increase in traffic on lanes and roads that were not designed for it and cannot cope. This in turn leads to 'road improvement schemes' — by-passes, road widening, straightening of bends — all of which speed up the flow of traffic and encourage further inmigration as rural areas become accessible to ever more distant conurbations.

Road improvement also feeds back into property development in another less obvious way. It is in fact one of the spearheads of rural urbanisation, for it degrades the land around it, making it less attractive and so easier for speculative builders and planners to connive at growth. The county town by-pass is a good example. This usually cuts a metalled swathe through fields at some distance from the town itself. As soon as this happens, the land within the compass of the by-pass is ripe for development.

In terms of the amount of land consumed alone, the urbanisation of the countryside is a serious problem. I know of no overall figures for Wales, but a report published by the Council for the Protection of Rural England in 1992 gives a good indication of the scale of land loss to development.

According to the CPRE, 460 square miles of England were built over in the 1980s, while between 1945 and 1990 land lost to development was 2,720 square miles, which is an area greater than Greater London, Berkshire, Hertfordshire and Oxfordshire. About fifteen per cent of England is now urban, a figure which the CPRE estimates will increase to twenty per cent in the next fifty years if present trends continue.[5]

Land loss to urbanisation on this scale has obvious environmental consequences. But the spread of an urban environment throughout the countryside has another effect which is not easy to quantify although its repercussions may be profound. Since this is also bound up with tourism, however, I will turn to the latter first.

*

We are constantly reminded in the press that tourism is now a major Welsh 'industry' employing 95,000 people or nine per cent of the workforce, with an annual turnover of some £1.3 billion. Tourism, we're urged to agree, is a 'good thing', helping to provide jobs in hard-pressed rural areas (as well as in some derelict industrial ones) and enabling hill farmers to eke out a living at a time of agricultural crisis.

As with so much else in machine culture however, tourism's success brings us up against questions of scale. Wales has had its tourists for over two hundred years but in numbers that were manageable. The curious English who tramped the hills and shores, who botanized or bathed, were early (unintentional) examples of 'sustainable' or 'green' tourism in the modern jargon. On the whole they neither disrupted communities nor degraded nature.

The situation now is very different. When hundreds of thousands of people press into Wales each summer week, even the most environmentally conscious tourist becomes intrusive, and most tourists are nothing of the sort. Most, like the retirees of Norton, come for the 'beautiful countryside' and possibly a 'bit of local colour'. The intricacies of Welsh society and culture are of no interest to them, and since large areas of Wales still do look beautiful, there's little reason for the tourist on a fortnight's holiday to speculate that this appearance may be superficial.

The truth is mass tourism is a corrosive phenomenon, degrading the host society and nature. A nation that depends on tourism as Wales now does must learn to manipulate its culture. In the words of Tony Lewis, chairman of the Wales Tourist Board, it must create and sell an image of itself.[6] Such an 'image' is a lie, of course. This doesn't matter to the WTB and others involved in the hard sell of Wales, any more than its consequence. Hyped at home and abroad, it feeds back into society, especially since the tourist who has bought the image expects to find it reflected in our streets and hills, on our faces and lips. The 'industry' — meaning ever increasing numbers of Welsh people — must comply. Mass tourism demands servility and passivity of its hosts in return for its money.

The degradation of nature through tourism is only now being recognised for the problem it is, and only with reluctance on the part of the 'industry' which would rather talk of growth, job creation and increased turnover. Under pressure from environmental organisations, however, we can expect to see a significant increase in the coupling of 'green' and 'sustainable' with 'tourism' in the promotional literature of the tourist organisations. But while these organisations continue to push for the growth of tourism, this can be no more than window dressing.

A major problem is that those areas most attractive in Wales from the point of view of tourist exploitation are also amongst the most vulnerable ecologically. They include dune and cliff ecosystems along the coasts and the large tracts of upland moors.[7] Such areas cannot sustain large concentrations of people and many have already been extensively damaged by increased tourism in the last twenty-five years.

The Black Mountains in Gwent provide an example. When they first began to be exploited for their tourist potential in the mid to late 1960s, the idea of any environmental impact was dismissed by those with vested interests. Tourism would create jobs and bring badly needed income into an already depressed rural community. Twenty-five years on, a European seminar on 'sustainable tourism' was held in the Llanthony Valley in the Mountains, the valley itself providing a focus for the nexus of problems — ecological, economic and social — that beset fragile rural environments in the face of mass tourism.[8]

In the Llanthony Valley traffic has become a major problem, for the narrow lane that threads along it cannot cope with the increasing numbers of cars that converge on the area in summer. Suggestions that passing places should be improved would only compound the problem. For in the valley, as elsewhere, improved roads would merely encourage more traffic. As it is, the volume of traffic causes degradation of hedge banks due to the constant undermining of their base as cars edge into them in the confined space. (There could never be sufficient passing places to solve this problem on such a narrow, winding and long lane.) Inevitably too, more cars have meant more litter which has now become an annual nuisance to the residents of the valley.

There is an irony in all this as well, since though tourism has helped degrade the valley, it has not had any appreciable effect on its economic problems. Farming has continued to decline but because of the nature of tourism in the area, income has not been supplemented from the tourist trade to any significant degree. At the European conference held in the valley, John Aitchison of the International Centre for Protected Landscapes at University College of Wales Aberystwyth noted that "Fifty per cent of farms in the valley are not having any identifiable success, and there is the possibility that the whole valley could break up and collapse, possibly within five to ten years".[9]

From the point of view of the tourist, of course, none of this is important because it is not even apparent. Most visit the valley, as they do other beautiful areas of Wales, for the scenery, and driving from Cwmyoy to Capel-y-ffin it is possible to believe that nothing has changed in the Black Mountains for generations and that nothing could change.

To apprehend the extent of environmental damage due to increased tourist and recreational use, you need to climb out of the valley into the surrounding hills. Even then it is necessary to have some idea of how the Black Mountains looked forty years ago.

The main forms of tourism and recreation in the Black Mountains are pony trekking, walking, hang-gliding and, more recently, mountain bike and motorcycle riding. None of these involves large numbers of people and it is possible to walk the ridges all day if you're lucky and not see more than a few fellow walkers or a string of pony trekkers in the distance. But their cumulative effect over a quarter of a century has meant, to take one example, the disappearance of large numbers of the springy, cropped mountain grass tracks that forty years ago criss-crossed the hills. When you come across one now in an out-of-the-way place it seems like a memento from the past. The grass was rapidly cut to pieces by ponies' hooves, tramped bare by walkers, churned by motorcycles. There is never time for it to recover. In summer the more popular tracks on the ridges are powdered peat dust, in winter caked mud; where tracks descend to the valleys, run-off from the slopes after rain has eroded them to a rocky rubble formed from the underlying sandstone, on which it is difficult to walk. On very popular routes, such as the ascent of the Sugar Loaf from Abergavenny, the path has been obliterated into a broad area of devastation near the summit, as walkers move further and further to the sides in search of a more pleasant ascent. What was a narrow green path forty years ago is now a pale brown rocky gash visible from the town over three miles away.

The more popular tracks within walking distance of Abergavenny have also been staked out as 'walks' with numbered poles at intervals along the way for the convenience of visitors. Little by little the hills are becoming tamed, suburbanised like our villages, to conform to the expectations of Britain's suburban culture. The Black Mountains, like many areas of rural Wales that not so long ago were quiet and fairly remote, are being turned into an agreeable green park for the purposes of 'recreation'. They are being trivialised, as they were bound to be with the rapid intrusion of tourism, for we are part of a culture that encourages trivial lives.

*

Suburbanisation is in fact one of the greatest threats to the environment in Wales, as elsewhere in the industrialised world. For it is more than the sum of its physical manifestations — the 'suburbs' — it is a state of mind which seeks to replicate itself wherever it goes. So even in remote villages and isolated cottages you are likely to find lifestyles and attitudes little different from those in a great conurbation.

Its success is due in part to the suburban mind's great pioneering spirit. There has hardly been a period in the history of Wales when the countryside was changed so rapidly and radically and with such energy and enthusiasm. Road building, road improvement, malls and arcades, out-of-town hypermarkets, estates and in-filling, bungalows and theme parks — for the suburban mind what is left of nature is the last frontier, to be vigorously assailed.

But it might be asked how this squares with apparent public concern over the environment — from general phenomena such as global warming to the particulars of species conservation. The answer, I believe, is that most people don't think about the environment most of the time and even fewer relate their own behaviour to environmental problems to the extent that they change their way of life. That is, change it radically. For though many make small adjustments that are not inconvenient and may even save money (such as loft insulation and double glazing), very few make changes in their way of living that are actually inconvenient and which would be judged by society in general as retrograde — like giving up the car.

Part of the reason for this is that the suburban mind is isolated against much of the reality of environmental degradation. Periodically the media give rise to mass anxiety over environmental problems, but this always peaks and the mind's attention strays or is enticed elsewhere. For the media it was a story; once its news value has diminished it is dropped. Looking out of the window of the house or the car, for most of the time it is possible to think that things are not so bad after all.

There is a 'dead-hand' in the human mind which cuts us off from contemplating too much reality and which leaves environmental groups with an unresolved dilemma. In 1992 the RSPB launched a promotional 'Campaign for the Countryside', designed to increase public awareness of the rapid decline in bird species in Britain due (largely) to changes in farming methods. For anyone interested in birds the litany of loss is a familiar one. In Wales alone: *corn bunting*, severely reduced; *lapwing*, declined by fifty-two per cent in a decade; *curlew*, declined by thirteen per cent in the 1980s; *snipe*, declined by sixty per cent; *hen harrier*, down to eleven breeding pairs in 1991; *red grouse*, reduced to 900 pairs for the whole of Wales; *linnet*, once common, now becoming rare. One could go on.

Farming methods, as mentioned above, are the main cause of this disastrous decline, but we should add all the road-building projects, new estates and green-site factories associated with urbanisation, the pollution from human effluent, human encroachment on nesting and feeding grounds such as sand dunes, estuarine mud flats, broad-leaf woods and moors.

In one of its campaign information sheets the RSPB talks of making "a countryside fit for birds and people". It is a line often taken by environmentally concerned groups (reflecting a need they feel to strike an uneasy balance between conservation and human use) which identifies but does not confront the real dilemma. Announcing the Dee Estuary Strategy in 1992, for instance, the Dee Estuary Forum, English Nature and the Countryside Council for Wales proclaimed in a joint press release that "It is our objective to provide a strategy which has the vision and foresight to safeguard and enhance the nature conservation value of our estuaries whilst recognising the wide range of human pressures placed upon them". What are the pressures on this major European site for over-wintering wading birds? "...leisure, tourism, development, industry, shipping, pollution..." A Countryside Council for Wales press release of January 1993, announcing that it had been asked by the Welsh Office to sound out public opinion on the proposed designation of the Menai Strait as a Marine Nature Reserve, states: "The varied rock and sediment habits of the Strait support a wide range of interesting and unusual marine and coastal wildlife". But, "While highlighting the value of the area, CCW realises that the Strait has a commercial and amenity value for many local people and visitors". Moreover, Mike Gash, marine and coast policy officer for the CCW, is quoted: "It has been suggested that the reserve would curtail people's rights. In fact, the Wildlife and Countryside Act of 1981 states specifically that nothing may be done in a Marine Nature Reserve which would infringe the rights of any individual or body. So there is no chance for example, that sailing or angling could be prohibited". Instead "voluntary agreements" will be sought to regulate "some activities".

All three statements make the same point — conservation of habitat and protection of species are in conflict with the demands of human use. All three duly make an about-turn to suggest that (in some vague way) they can be reconciled.

But past experience suggests that this is not so. There are too many people making too many demands on the environment, and human interest is almost always going to take precedent. There will be a concerted attempt by a minority to preserve, for example, diversity of habitat and bird species, but this will be in opposition to the demands of the urbanised many for whom the countryside is no more than a playground. The interest of the majority in nature goes little beyond that. Reading of the imminent demise of the corn bunting as a Welsh species, the individual may pause and feel regret, but most have never seen a corn bunting and would mistake it for a sparrow if they did. Loss of species really means very little, because in our suburbanised environment corn bunting, lapwing, linnet and curlew are scarcely more than names. They have not been internalised as a necessary part of our world.

For this reason alone, conservationists are limited to a rearguard action, arousing public interest when they can, saving a pond here, a wood there, but always in retreat, with every gain provisional and liable to be reversed. The attrition of supposedly inviolable Sites of Special Scientific Interest should convince us of this. And most of us will go along with it, putting short-term human interest first, only fitfully aware that things are badly wrong as we seek distraction in the new Wales while it lasts — the grand-scale suburban park.

Notes

1. Statistics and quotation from Henry Kendall are taken from Margaret Holloway, 'Population Pressure', *Scientific American* (September 1992); also Henry C. Tuckwell and James A. Koziol, 'World Population', *Nature* 359 (17 September 1992).
2. Margaret Keenan, 'Millions Dream of Moving to the Country', *Western Mail* (2 November 1992).
3. Clive Betts, 'English Migrants Taking Over Districts', *Western Mail* (3 November 1992). The significance of this for the Welsh language heartlands of Dyfed and Gwynedd is clear. See John Aitchison and Harold Carter, 'The Welsh Language in 1991 — A Broken Heartland and a New Beginning?', *Planet* 97 (1993).
4. 'New Homes for Newcomers?', *Rural Wales/Cymru Wledig* (Autumn 1992).
5. As reported by Nicholas Schoon, 'Growing Concern Over Britain's Disappearing Land', *The Independent* (16 October 1992).
6. Michael Boon, 'Opening the Batting for Wales', *Western Mail* (26 October 1992).
7. Neil Ravenscroft, 'The Environmental Impact of Recreation and Tourism', *European Environment Magazine*, 1992.
8. David Vickerman, 'Valley on a Knife-Edge', *Western Mail* (6 November 1992).
9. As reported by David Vickerman, cited above.

Rory Francis

Transport in Wales: Coming In or Going Out?

1. Tongues of Tarmac

In an article in 1993 for the magazine *Dan Haul*, Merfin Williams referred to the roads of Wales as "Tafodau Tarmac", tongues of tarmac, progressively devouring the countryside, moulding our lives and creating, over the years, a country very different to the one we have known.

Of course, there are very few people indeed who are against roads as such. Whether we are discussing Sarn Helen, the routes of the drovers, or the A55 Expressway, they are imperative expressions of communication. It should be stated that the circuitous, occasionally mysterious lanes of rural Clwyd, Dyfed and the Vale of Glamorgan, banked by high hedges and followed by ditches and dry stone walls, contribute to and not reduce, the quality of the local environment. They certainly have a historical importance. Neither can environmentalists claim that all new roads are bad roads. A notorious bottleneck, such as that which used to occur at Conwy before the road-tunnel was constructed, can create serious environmental and social problems. From the Bronze Age trackways of Preseli to the concrete maw of the M4 as it disgorges its traffic into and out of Wales, roads are the most potent images of how we live. The predicament now, however, is that it is roads that increasingly control the quality of our lives and threaten a profound deterioration to both the urban and the rural landscape.

The 1990s have been hailed as the decade of environmentalism, the decade when businesses and governments across the world are beginning to reassess their priorities in the light of new green awareness. In certain fields that may be partially true. In the area of transport, in Wales at least, that new thinking seems to be a long way off.

A few statistics. There are over 33,000 kilometres of roads in Wales, a figure that increased by six per cent during the eighties. In 1990, the Department of Transport estimates that vehicles travelled over 12.5 billion kilometres on major Welsh roads. For the UK as a whole, government forecasts suggest that between now and the year 2025 there will be an increase in road traffic of between 85 and 140 per cent. In other words, more or less two cars for every one today.

The absolute numbers are difficult to visualise, but this projected total of vehicles on British roads in 2025 would fill a London to Edinburgh motorway bumper to bumper — if it were 257 lanes wide.

The view persists, however, that such dire forecasts need not worry us in Wales, that we are (outside the south-east and north-east at least) a sparsely populated country, with huge amounts of spare capacity on our rural roads. The evidence we have suggests the opposite.

In 1992 the Transport Research Unit of Oxford University produced a study for the Countryside Commission in England, examining how the Department of Transport's traffic growth forecasts could possibly be realised. Their conclusion, broadly, was that there was limited scope for very major traffic growth within towns and cities themselves. Thus many roads are already over capacity.

However, if forecast growth levels do become a reality, this will in all likelihood be a result of a gradual spreading out of the conurbations, as wealthy commuters turn their backs on the towns where they earn their living, and move to distant suburbs and villages. This would imply a sustained increase in urban sprawl, a sort of 'Californication' of our countryside.

In terms of transport it would mean a truly massive increase in rural traffic. The TRU study suggests we could see between two and four cars on rural roads by 2025 for every one now. This would clearly imply a major alteration in the way we live. In many ways we have already become, as E.F. Schumacher wrote, a "footloose society", insatiable consumers of mobility, hopping ceaselessly from place to place, eternally convinced that things will be better wherever we are going next.

Massive changes have taken place over the last four decades in how and why we travel. Clearly this is a world trend which has global consequences for the environment. It is the result, in large measure, of a common interest held by the world's two largest industrial interests, the petroleum and the automotive industries. In Britain this cosy relationship has been supported explicitly by government over forty years, but never more enthusiastically than by the Conservative government over the last fifteen.

Mrs Thatcher believed that you could not stop the "great car economy". The truth is that the motor car was the sacred cow of the materialist eighties, symbolising freedom, macho culture, and a lack of concern for the environment. The legacy it has left is what Greenpeace calls 'Mad Car Disease', the government policy of never ending and uncritical support for motor interests, and the directing of the lion's share of transport spending into road building, thus starving the alternatives of investment.

Yet this growth in car ownership and use is not something which has been foisted on an unwilling populace by government action alone. We should not doubt that many of the 1.2 million private car owners in Wales are extremely attached to their vehicles. What is most worrying is that all too often, we allow this attachment to blind us to true costs which mass car use has upon our society and our environment.

In 1990, 244 people, almost a jumbo-jet-full, were killed on Welsh roads. A further 16,184 were injured. One murder, for example, will receive hours of coverage on national television, not to mention attention by the tabloid media. In contrast, the accidental death of a cyclist, hit by car, might at the most be mentioned in a local newspaper.

More insidious is the daily impact of vehicle emissions on our health. In 1988, road transport was responsible for eighty-eight per cent of emissions of carbon monoxide, forty-six per cent of nitrogen oxides, thirty-seven per cent of volatile organic compounds and nineteen per cent of carbon dioxide.

The link between vehicular air pollution and ill-health is a strong one. Ground level ozone (a secondary pollutant formed from nitrogen dioxide) is associated with eye, nose and throat irritation, chest discomfort, coughs, headaches and asthma. Hydrocarbons, especially benzene, are known to cause cancer. In fact, benzene is considered so dangerous to human health that the World Health Organisation is unwilling to set 'safe' limits. Carbon monoxide is clearly proven to be injurious to health. These emissions are created by motor traffic, and are to be found in increasingly higher levels in the air, especially in our towns and cities.

The American Lung Association has estimated that up to 30,000 premature deaths a year are caused in the USA by vehicular pollution, whilst in Britain the number of asthma sufferers is increasing by five per cent a year. Yet as with most pollution, the risks are not evenly distributed. Most at risk are children under five, the elderly, unborn babies and those prone to asthma — around twenty per cent of the population.

In summer 1990, the City of Cardiff invested in a state-of-the-art 'OPSIS' spectrometer. This is able to give regular up-to-the-minute readings for four of the most significant pollutant gases. Within weeks of its being installed, the findings had hit the headlines. They showed that central Cardiff was suffering levels of ground ozone pollution higher than the guideline level given by the World Health Organisation.

Reactions to this sort of air pollution across the world vary widely. In Vienna and Amsterdam, cars are being gradually banned from the city centre. In Mexico City, oxygen is being sold in telephone boxes at $2 a shot. Yet in South Glamorgan there appears to have been little reaction at all to unacceptable pollution levels: new roads continue to be planned and built, multi-storey car parks spring up in the city centre and public transport is left under-funded.

Of course there is one ray of hope — for some. This is the use of catalytic converters. All new cars must now have these bolt-on devices to treat exhaust emissions of nitrous oxides and carbon monoxide. But a catalytic converter only reaches full efficiency after approximately two miles of operation. Yet around half of all journeys are under five miles. In the 1992 updated White Paper *This Common Inheritance*, the Government accepted that despite government action to require catalytic converters on new small cars "much of the benefit of these measures risks being lost through continued growth in traffic volume and congestion" (p.101). Moreover, catalysts increase, not cut, vehicular emissions of carbon dioxide, the major greenhouse gas.

Nor are the consequences of a car-based economy limited to the purely physical aspects of life. There is increasing concern about the effects of new road building on Welsh speaking communities. The opening up of the A55 Expressway in the north has been a boost to tourism, bringing Caernarfon within a seventy-five minute journey from Merseyside. This does not merely encourage tourism, but opens up North Wales to commuters from Merseyside and Chester who wish to live in the Conwy valley or even further west. As a result, local people, perhaps first-time buyers, are having to compete in the housing market with outsiders with a higher disposable income, and at a time when the alternatives to owner-occupation have seldom been more limited.

Exactly what the effect of the new A55 will be on the Welsh-language strongholds of Gwynedd, is probably too early to say. Yet perhaps the time has come for the Welsh Office and local authorities concerned to take up the suggestion made by Twm Elias of Plas Tan y Bwlch, and commission not only an environmental impact assessment of major new road schemes, but a cultural impact assessment as well.

2. The Twyford Factor

It is clear that government road building policies are also on a crash course with the nature conservation movement. The National Roads Programme in England will effect 1,500 wildlife sites, over 500 sites of ancient woodland[1], 161 Sites of Special Scientific Interest, the very best of English wildlife sites. The figure in Wales is not known, but the enormity of modern road building dictates that there will be major destruction. For example, it takes twenty-five acres of land and 250,000 tonnes of gravel to build one mile of motorway.

Currently in Wales the most striking example of this is the Gwenlais Valley, Dyfed. Alfred McAlpine Quarry Products Ltd wish to start working on an old quarry, Cilyrychen, and destroy an area of land containing four SSSIs. The only known 'turlough' (a lake formed from an undiscovered source) in the British Isles, outside of Ireland, could well be badly affected. It is thought that road building would be the major outlet for the stone quarried.

Examples of wildlife areas in Wales under threat from road building are not difficult to find. The proposed Carmarthen by-pass would destroy part of the Bishop's Pond SSSI, an ox-bow lake in the flood plain of the River Tywi. In Snowdonia the Welsh Office has declared its intention to 'improve' the A5 near the Padog bends, by building over land owned by the National Trust, and held by them in order that it may be preserved on behalf of the nation. The Trust's Chief Executive has stated that the body is unlikely to agree to surrender the land for road building, and it is quite possible that the matter will have to be resolved in court.

The very day (8 July 1993) after the Department of Transport in England announced it was dropping plans for a motorway through Oxleas Wood in London, because it would have meant damaging one SSSI, the Welsh Office opened a public exhibition on their plans for twenty-two kilometres of new motorway across the Gwent Levels. This would mean bulldozing through six SSSIs. Some observers commented, unkindly, that if the Welsh Office has a sixth of the concern for the environment as the Department of Transport in England, they would also abandon their scheme.

The new motorway, effectively a duplicate M4 (actually the 'M48') through Gwent, would link the new Severn Bridge to the existing M4 at Castleton, thus encircling Newport in a M25-style grip. The countryside under threat, the Gwent Levels, is unique in Wales. Reclaimed by the Romans, it is noted for its many drainage ditches or 'reens', which support a wealth of wildlife including no less than 115 nationally rare species. The official attitude, however, is that the requirements of 'development' are paramount, and that other considerations have to be subservient to that.

Interestingly, the two latter proposed M48 routes also cut through part of the proposed Severn Estuary Special Protection Area. SPAs are declared under European law, with the aim of protecting internationally important wildlife sites. In effect, they prevent all development within an area which would have wide-spread ecological harm, unless it is necessary to protect human life — such as flood defence.

Other 'nightmare' road schemes in Wales include the so-called Euro-routes, planned by the EU as part of a European trunk road network. The British section of the plan has been put together by the Department of Transport in London, with scant reference to the Welsh Office, which has responsibility for roads in Wales. As well as a Gwent to Pembrokeshire road, most of which already exists as the M4, the plan includes a more or less motorway-standard road from Shrewsbury to Bangor, through the Snowdonia National Park. However, the prospect of a six-lane highway running alongside Nant Ffrancon, or of Betws y Coed shadowed by a motorway fly-over was too much even for the Welsh Office. To his credit, Sir Wyn Roberts, the then Welsh Office Roads Minister, appeared to have ruled the scheme out absolutely. Yet the overall Euro-route plan still exists, and under a different minister some time in the future, Wales could once again be pressured to accept it.

3. Thinking Globally

Important as these problems are, they are all local or regional in character. We should not forget that road transport is heavily implicated in global warming, and that we are interfering in ways we do not fully understand with the earth's climatic system. Six of the hottest years this century have occurred since 1981. Scientists believe that under a 'business as usual' regime world temperatures will rise three to four degrees centigrade above the current levels by 2100. Meanwhile, road transport is already the largest and fastest-growing energy-using sector in Britain. (It accounts for fifty per cent of the seventy million tonnes of oil we use each year).

The UN's experts on climate change, the International Panel on Climate Change, are certain that global warming is taking place, and have recommended that emissions of greenhouse gases be cut by twenty per cent. World leaders have baulked at that suggestion, offering only to stabilise emissions at current levels. Yet even that target may elude Britain, largely because of the growth of road transport.

One might presume, therefore, that a major rethink might have started, and that academics, the general public, even politicians, have begun to realise that our dependence on the car is too damaging to sustain. Far from it. The recession of 1990 to 1993 led to a flurry of calls from across the political spectrum for special measures to revive the motor industry — the 'barometer of the health of the economy'. Likewise, most people seem to have accepted that it is in some sense 'normal' to poison the air which we breathe with exhaust gases, to destroy some of our most precious wildlife sites, and to threaten the equilibrium of the world's climatic system.

Yet there are hopeful signs, indeed a stirring which will hopefully lead to real action for a coherent UK transport system. In southern England, the determination with which the respectable citizens of Winchester fought to save the small area of open hillside named Twyford Down has given inspiration to campaigners across Britain and beyond. The land, a designated SSSI including notable Iron Age remains, had been bequeathed to Winchester School on the strict condition that it would be protected as open heathland. But that made little impression on the Department of Transport's engineers, who were set on driving the motorway through the site, with the aim of making the journey from London to Southampton three minutes shorter.

There was never any doubt the local community opposed the scheme, and national groups such as Friends of the Earth went to the European Court in an attempt to halt construction. But what left the strongest impression on many were the attempts by the Dongas, young people who adopted a 'tribal' name from the ravaged Iron Age footways of the downs. These people, foolishly dismissed by the DoT as 'trouble-makers' or 'New Age Travellers', camped on the site to challenge the bulldozers in the most direct fashion possible. In reality, their efforts were defeated, yet their influence has been seminal for the whole of the UK environmental movement, and also for many 'unaligned' members of the public, possessed of no great environmental knowledge, but nevertheless appalled at the implications of the Government's £12 billion roads programme.

Twyford Down is not in Wales. But people from Wales took part in attempting to defend this unique area of English chalk downland. This is as politically as it is environmentally significant. These individuals have brought their experiences and impressions back to Wales, where precisely the same highway madness is threatening our countryside, from Snowdonia to the Gwent Levels, from Carmarthen to the Vale of Clwyd.

4. Cardiff — a case study

There are signs that in Wales ideas are beginning to change. In Autumn 1991, Cardiff Friends of the Earth were disturbed to discover the transport implications of the update of the South Glamorgan Structure Plan. County Council officials were anticipating not merely a doubling of traffic within twenty-five years, in line with government predictions. They were planning for an additional thirty per cent increase as a result of the development of Cardiff Bay — all told, an astonishing growth of a hundred and sixty per cent.

To accommodate this deluge of traffic, the county council planned to build seven miles of new dual carriageway, plus the completion of its flagship "Peripheral Distributor Route" through the south of the city, at a cost of £135 million. Thus after a major fund raising exercise, the volunteers of Cardiff FoE commissioned consultants from Transport and Environmental Studies (TEST) to draw up an alternative vision for how transport in the city could work — a blueprint for green transport in Cardiff. This suggested a 50:50 "model split" between the private car and other forms of transport within the city. At present there is a 60:40 bias in favour of the car.

The Cardiff proposed in the TEST Report would be a different city from the one with which we are familiar. Rail services would be markedly improved. A line would be relain between Radyr and Coryton, recreating a rail loop. The Butetown rail link, from central Cardiff to the docks would be restored, thus repairing the damage shortly to be inflicted by the Cardiff Bay Development Corporation, which plans to tear up the existing railway and replace it with a wide *boulevard*. The usefulness of this line would be further enhanced by completing a rail loop from Butetown eastwards towards St. Mellons. The speed and reliability of buses would be boosted by the creation of bus lanes along all the major arterial routes into Cardiff: Newport Road, North Road, Cowbridge Road

East and Penarth Road.

For cyclists, a network of cycle routes would be created across the city. Cycling is not merely beneficial to the environment (if it replaces other forms of transport). It is also good for health. People who cycle twenty miles a week have half the risk of suffering from coronary heart disease of those who do not, and the British Medical Association has recently adopted a policy of enthusiastic support for the promotion of cycling. Nationally, sales of bikes have rocketed in recent years, usually outstripping those of cars, but many cyclists are intimidated by traffic levels. The TEST Report proposed setting a target of five per cent of trips within the city being made by bicycle. The present figure is a derisory one per cent.

The major inner city residential areas of Cardiff — Canton, Pontcanna, Roath and Splott, which suffer greatly from traffic noise and speeding cars at present, would be offered relief. Cross area traffic calming schemes would be introduced, cutting speed limits to twenty miles per hour, and changing the design of streets imaginatively so as to encourage drivers to maintain low speeds. Traffic calming on this scale would have a double benefit. Not only would it directly reduce danger, reintroducing the idea that streets primarily belong to people; it would also reduce the relative effectiveness of the motor car as a way of travelling through the inner city urban area, giving a corresponding boost to the train, the bus and the bicycle.

The report has attracted a good deal of support. (It should be remembered that forty per cent of families in the city do not possess a car.) As to funding the changes, the TEST Report suggested that major new roads planned by the county council would simply not be necessary given the switch towards public transport which was being proposed. The scrapping of these roads would save the council an estimated £35-40 million, enough in theory to put into effect most of the ideas in the report, without increasing council tax.

Radical as the ideas in the TEST Report may seem, a broadly similar plan has already been adopted by Central Region in Scotland. Here, a new policy document, titled 'All Change', outlines a fifteen year spending programme allocating £14 million to pedestrian facilities, £5-7 million to improved rail links, £9 million to better provision for buses, £3 million to bicycle facilities and £10 million to traffic calming. The same document details £30 million of road and parking schemes which are being deleted from the structure plan.

It is thus possible to change transport policies, given the will at local level. However, whether such a plan could be completely imitated in Wales is questionable, as most of the major county council road schemes here are funded by the Welsh Office.

5. Greater Access, Less Mobility

Underlining the whole transport debate is the simple but neglected truth that what individuals demand is access — to the workplace, the school, the library, the shopping centre and the countryside. In a democratic society no one would suggest that such access should be denied. What causes the environmental problems is not access but mobility. Yet mobility is simply the means to an end, not the end itself.

Traditionally, towns and cities were planned, of necessity, in this way. Before the age of mass car ownership, major services had to be located in areas which could possibly be reached. This in turn provided natural nodes for the public transport system. Over the last twenty years this model has begun to disintegrate.

The main growth area for the retail trade has been in big out-of-town stores, often accessible only by car. Likewise, football clubs, small businesses and even county councils have been lured by the attractions of sites outside the town centre. As a result the majority who do not have exclusive access to cars, which includes all children and a high proportion of the elderly, have been isolated. Those who possess private transport are therefore forced to use it — and those without vehicles are pressured to obtain them. Such a *laissez-faire* approach to planning has a powerful effect in encouraging people to adopt an environmentally unsustainable lifestyle.

The solution lies in intelligent use of the planning system — deciding where the major business centres are to be located, and ensuring they can be well served by public transport. The local authorities have been quicker than central government in recognising the benefits of this approach. The Welsh Office has now published a Planning Guidance Note for local authorities (PPG 6 Revised) which states that out-of-town retail developments should not be of a scale such as to "trigger a long-term decline in those town and neighbourhood centres which would otherwise serve the community well". Progress indeed. We shall have to see what this means in practice.

Thus the first principle of transport planning should be to attempt to reduce actual journey numbers. But many trips are essential. The emphasis therefore should be to encourage the use of transport modes which do less environmental damage. Yet government policy has consistently committed the lion's share of the transport budget to road building and maintenance.

Comparisons of spending in Wales are difficult to make, as the government's grant to British Rail is made on an all-Britain basis. But in 1991-92 the Department of Transport invested £1.8 billion in the major road network, but less than £800 million in public transport. To make matters worse, BR was forbidden by government rules from borrowing money for investment unless it could show a likely return of eight per cent — a target few private companies could meet, especially during lean years of recession. Privatisation, for reasons which will be explored later, is unlikely to improve the situation.

The stock response in the past has been that the Treasury receives more money in car and fuel taxes than it spends on the road programme. It is a powerful argument, but one which does not stand up under scrutiny. Like so much traditional economics it simply ignores the 'externalities', the very real costs which car and lorry use impose on society, but which are not paid by the motorist. Whitelegg has reworked these calculations, but included the cost of accidents, pollution, congestion and global warming, and concluded that private motoring taxes only cover twenty-seven per cent of the costs so imposed on society. The equivalent figure for HGVs is only twenty-three per cent.[2]

The Government should therefore not be over-cautious about increasing motor taxes, be that through fuel taxes or charging motorists for the use of motorways or over-congested city-centres. I would suggest, however, that such measures would be more likely to be understood and supported if they were introduced at the same time as an integrated and well-financed policy to improve public transport.

However, organisations such as the Wales Tourist Board claim that environmentalists should be enthusiastic supporters of certain new road building. By this they mean by-passes, which are claimed to offer relief to small towns and villages suffering from congestion, road damage and air pollution. As usual, fact is more complex than rhetoric.

For example, a number of so-called by-passes are in fact 'links in a chain' of new major roads. An extreme example of this is the Folkestone to Honiton Trunk road in southern England, which is composed of over twenty-one by-passes strung together. Thankfully there is nothing similar to this in Wales, but every by-pass built has the effect of making that particular long-distance route a little quicker and easier, which in the longer term can only encourage more traffic.

Here we might briefly examine the case of Bethesda, on Telford's A5 in the Ogwen Valley in Snowdonia. The Welsh Office proposed a by-pass, a proposal which is supported by some of the local councillors in the belief it will improve traffic conditions in the town. But the by-pass, along with the planned 'up-grading' of the A5 at the Padog bends further west, will have the effect of making the A5 through Snowdonia a more attractive one for long distance, Shrewsbury to Bangor traffic.

There is now a perfectly good long-distance alternative to the A5 in the recently completed A55 Expressway, a Welsh Office flagship road. The risk is that if the Bethesda by-pass is built, and the A5 up-graded, then traffic levels through Snowdonia will grow even faster than elsewhere, and the environmental pressure on the whole area increase.

By-passes may partially relieve one area, but actually make things worse along the major road concerned. What is needed is a 'whole route approach', looking at options for managing traffic along a considerable stretch of road, not merely a small section of it.

The proponents of by-passes have also frequently over-estimated the benefit they can have, by forgetting how much traffic is entirely local in character. In Bethesda, sixty-seven to seventy-five per cent of traffic entering the town has been shown to be local.[3] This is not surprising, bearing in mind that most journeys are under five miles, and that population levels along the A5 south of Bethesda are extremely low. It means, however, that a by-pass could be used by a maximum of twenty-five to thirty-three per cent of traffic passing through the town. That is the kind of reduction which could be cancelled out in a few short years if overall car use continues to rise unabated.

Wales certainly has important transport needs, but building ever more roads is not the way to meet them. The answer, if we want an efficient and environmentally sustainable system, lies in integration — making sure that public transport is supported and that it meshes together effectively with other modes.

To the passenger, the most attractive form of public transport is the train. And from an environmental perspective, rail is usually the most energy-efficient form of public transport. But in Wales our rail network is a shadow of its former self. In 1922 it was possible to travel by rail directly from Merthyr to Llanidloes, from Dolgellau to Ruabon, and from Porthmadog to Caernarfon. When the Maesteg to Cardiff line was reopened in 1992, thanks to a grant from Mid Glamorgan County Council, it proved so popular with the public that projected passenger levels for its first four years were reached in the first month.

But much more could be made of our railways. Hopes of making the 1992 Ebbw Vale Garden Festival match its hyperbole as a truly green event, as it had been billed in its literature, were dashed when it became clear that it would not be possible to travel to the site by train, although a railway passes within a quarter of a mile. The track was only maintained to freight standards, and a grant to up-grade it for the big event was not forthcoming from Gwent County Council. The two million visitors came by road.

However, the Railways Development Society has put forward plans for up-grading the Welsh rail network, reopening the Carmarthen to Aberystwyth and the Bangor to Porthmadog lines. Rhodri Clarke has pointed out in the *Western Mail* that if the Caernarfon to Bangor line were reopened, it would be technically feasible to run a direct train from Cardiff to Caernarfon in three and three quarter hours. (A typical car journey would take one and a quarter hours more.)

Money will always be a problem in reopening railway lines. But if one considers the resources pumped into major road schemes, the price looks a great deal more affordable. Take the Carmarthen to Aberystwyth line. To relay this would cost up to £110 million —not significantly more than the threatened £95 million 'Ceredigion Link Roads' which would scar the Dyfed countryside from Carmarthen to Lampeter and Aberteifi. Yet the environmental savings would be enormous.

Another area where rail has clear advantages over road is in the transport of long distance bulk freight. But during the last few years there has been a virtual collapse in the proportion of freight in Wales being carried by rail. In 1989, rail freight in and out of Wales fell by thirteen and twenty-one per cent respectively. During the same year, the volume of goods exported from Wales by road went up by twenty-nine per cent. This can only partially be attributed to the decline of traditional industries. What is clear is that a freight distribution system which is so strongly road-based is neither sustainable nor environmentally acceptable. For example, one legally laden lorry causes the same amount of road damage as 100,000 cars. Yet the freight lobby continues to pressurise the Government and the EU to raise the top legal lorry weight limit from thirty-six to forty-four tonnes.

However, official thinking has been dominated not by an urge to boost support for our railways, but rather by privatisation. The point is not that private ownership is inherently a bad thing for railways — the pre-Beeching network was built up by private companies, while names such as Great Western still evoke enthusiasm and nostalgia. The concern of environmentalists is that the Government's real agenda is *not* to help bring about a major shift in transport from road to rail, but rather to cut back on financial support for the railways. It is these priorities that will determine what the overall outcome of privatisation will be.

The Government's desire to cut back on railway subsidies is not in doubt. BR's Public Service Obligation Grant was already reduced in real terms to fifteen per cent of its 1979 level, when a further cut of twenty-two per cent took place in 1993/94. Government ministers still defend the deregulation of buses on the basis of the savings it brought about in public sector support to the industry, forgetting that since deregulation bus patronage has plummeted, fares have increased and the usefulness of the service has declined as integrated time-tabling has disappeared.

The risk with privatisation is that the Government's priorities will inflict the same sort of damage as happened to the buses, and for the same reasons. In their enthusiasm to hive off substantial sections of the network to private operators, ministers will be tempted to relax their requirements on 'through ticketing' and integrated time-tabling. Concessionary cards will also be threatened. All of this will make rail less user-friendly.

More seriously threatened are the so-called 'marginal' routes such as the Heart of Wales and the Cambrian Coast lines. If the subsidies demanded by the operators to run these lines are considered too high, the likelihood is that they will close, doubtless following an expensive public enquiry. The contribution such lines could make to sensitive tourism developments is immense.

Regarding railways in south-east Wales, these would seem to be in a healthier state. An estimated 500,000 people travel by south-east Wales trains every year, whilst 15,000 use Cardiff-Valleys services each working day. The last ten years have seen an encouraging growth with the opening of twenty-four new stations.

There are plans for further improvements. West Glamorgan and Mid Glamorgan have already co-operated to reopen the Swansea to Bridgend route for local trains. More ambitiously, the Welsh Office have funded a study on the possibility of using light rail to link the fast-developing Cardiff Bay area with the Valley line network. This would allow a quarter hourly service, and could add hugely to the quality of life for those living and working in Cardiff Bay. The fate of such planning after local government reorganisation is unknown.

The Welsh Office's intention is that public transport responsibilities should pass to the new unitary authorities. But it does not appear realistic to expect authorities as small as Cardiff or Ogwr to take a strategic view of transport systems. Had Welsh local government reorganisation preceded the opening of the Maesteg line, it is difficult to imagine that Cardiff, the Vale of Glamorgan, the Glamorgan Valleys and Bridgend local councils would have worked together to fund the project.

Thus the Welsh Office should recognise that there is a pressing need to co-ordinate transport beyond the boundaries of individual boroughs, and that this would best be done by setting up a properly resourced Passenger Transport Executive to cover Glamorgan and Gwent. There is nothing revolutionary about this. PTEs exist already in the major conurbations of England and Scotland. Certainly they could do with greater resources and powers. But a PTE in south-east Wales could act as a focus in the task of luring drivers out of their cars.

Thus from Oxleas Wood to the Gwent Levels, from Twyford Down to Bethesda, people are waking up to the fact that our present transport habits, and today's transport system, are neither sustainable nor acceptable. Indeed, it is likely that in the next few years, the National Roads Programme, and the UK's lack of a coherent transport policy, will provoke the most widespread environmental campaign of direct action ever seen in the UK.

Post Script

The above was written in July 1993. Although, in essence, our dependence, indeed addiction, to unsustainable forms of transport remains the same, the last year has seen a major growth in the awareness of the problems of excessive car use. This has led, to a limited degree, to a number of minor changes in Government policy.

In January 1994, in the midst of growing concern about vehicle emissions and human ill-health, John Major launched 'Britain's Sustainability Strategy', the Government's attempt to translate commitments made at the 'Earth Summit' at Rio into practical policy. This document contained, for the first time ever, a commitment to implementing a strategy to limit the growth in road transport. Vague, certainly, but a step forward all the same.

In March 1994 John Redwood, the Secretary of State for Wales, announced a major review of road building in Wales. This included an explicit recognition that the A40 and the A5 across mainland Wales are no longer primary long distance routes, that these roads pass through extremely environmentally sensitive areas, and that 'improvements' on them in future will be made on safety grounds. As a result, the contentious Bethesda, Crickhowell and Abergavenny bypasses were either cancelled or indefinitely deferred.

On the downside, Mr Redwood was soon to announce that plans

to upgrade the M4 across South Wales would proceed, if anything, at even greater speed, despite the rejection of the whole idea by over eighty per cent of the respondents in the Welsh Office's own public consultation on these schemes. One example, certainly, of the public showing a far more intelligent and far sighted attitude than the politicians who are supposed to represent them.

Notes

1. 'Head-on Collision: Road building and wildlife in South East England', RSNC, 1990.
2. 'Till the Pips Squeak: Ecological Taxation Reform', paper presented by John Whitelegg to the Institute of British Geographers, 1991.
3. As recorded by Môn and Arfon Friends of the Earth on 14 and 18 August and 6 and 8 October 1992, and recorded in 'Traffic Calming in Bethesda and Crickhowell by Community and Environmental Planning', Friends of the Earth Cymru, November 1992.

Peter Midmore and Nic Lampkin

A Future for Welsh Agriculture

In Wales, as in most of the industrialised world, agriculture is of declining importance. It is still relatively more important than in Britain as a whole, contributing more to Gross Domestic Product, and employing a higher percentage of the workforce, though in general the resource-base which it depends on has never made it an easy industry in which to earn a living. There is a predominance of weathered, acid soils which are intrinsically less fertile than elsewhere; rainfall is high, terrain is hilly and farmland often steeply sloped; and farms are relatively small-sized. Despite the decline in economic importance, farming is still the major land using activity, and changes in activity are having important impacts on the environment, and on rural communities which depend primarily on agriculture as a source of livelihood. More dramatic changes may have occurred but for the intervention of governments and the EU in the markets for agricultural commodities, but it is now increasingly recognised that these actions, together with the pressure of commercial interests, have caused agriculture to perform against entirely different criteria than those which society and, latterly, the Government itself, require of it.

The need for sustainability is so widely accepted that it is now virtually a commonplace, and since the publication of the White Paper 'This Common Inheritance' (Department of the Environment, 1990), government action in every sphere has been tested against the benchmark which it provides. However, it is difficult to avoid the impression that anything other than lip service is being paid to the concept: it has become devalued from over-use, and is generally employed in any context where faint approbation is required. "Sustainable growth" for example, sounds good but has been divorced from any consideration of its original meaning and instead now represents GDP in the absence of inflationary impact.

At a conceptual level, it is easy to get away from the confusion surrounding sustainability; at a practical level, finding the means of implementing it are more difficult. The Brundtland Report (World Commission on Environment and Development, 1989) has defined sustainable development as meeting the needs of the present without compromising the ability of future generations to meet their own needs. The implications for agriculture, as a renewable source of food and fibre, are wide-ranging, and we make no apology for spelling these out in detail before getting to grips with the problem of how to apply any insights to the way in which agriculture is developing in Wales, and the way in which it *could* develop if more heed were paid to the heightened contemporary sense of environmental concern. The major principles are outlined below as a basis for subsequent discussion.

First, and perhaps most important, Brundtland's definition clearly states that we should meet the needs of the present generation. Though the main thrust of environmental concern about agriculture is to do with conservation of resources and their ability to meet food and other needs in the future, our current economic system fails to meet even the basic needs for food and fibre of between half and a third of the world's present population. Enough is *produced* to do so, but not in the right places, or under equitable trading conditions: as a consequence much is wasted. The countries of Western Europe import animal feedstuffs and hydrocarbons (either to produce agro-chemicals or to fuel mechanised farm operations) to grow food for which there is no internal market. The resulting surpluses are instead sold at highly subsidised prices which have the effect of de-stabilising the agricultural systems of the poorer countries of the world. This does not even have to be seen as a moral problem in order for it to present difficulties in securing sustainable agriculture in the future. The world's population is forecast to rise rapidly before stabilising in the middle of the next century. Even though the predictions may not, as a result of famine or disease, be fully realised, the struggle for resources is bound to intensify. That struggle may be less acute if we have in place a system of agricultural production which can readily adapt to the circumstances in which we are likely to find ourselves. Even better, by being able to divert resources to poorer countries, it may be possible to promote more sustainable systems there. The essence of the first principle is thus: a need for greater self-reliance, at appropriate levels of organisation; reduction of energy use; and reliance on systems which maximise output per unit of natural resource consumed.

Secondly, the concept of stewardship underlies the Brundtland definition of sustainability, as it counsels that the ability of future generations to meet their needs should be preserved. Without entering a debate about how we can know what those needs are likely to be, it is important to recognise that considerable impoverishment of the natural environment, on which people will have to depend more in future, has already occurred. That in turn implies the need to enhance and extend the existing natural endowment of forest and other vegetative cover, soils, marine environments and wildlife. It may be argued that with high and rising levels of world population, a densely populated Europe which is thrown back on its own resources cannot afford to indulge in conservation activities of this type. Far from being a luxury, however, conservation is essential. The green of the Welsh hills is a tribute, not to biodiversity, but to the skill of the plant and animal breeders. It is the uniform green of monocultural or at best bi-cultural systems, relying on hybrid clones of Sitka spruce, Italian ryegrass and the ewe or cow selected for survival in conditions which can be engineered to make it most prolific. Though small farms are less able to adopt the output-enhancing systems which are appropriate only on larger holdings, they are equally burdened with the consequences of falling prices as the support system is increasingly unwilling — or even unable — to absorb the increase in supplies. But though this specialisation has brought with it increasingly high yields, it has not correspondingly increased returns to agriculture in the long run, for costs have risen in more than proportion. At least in part, this may be attributed to the fact that the more specialised systems neglect beneficial interactions between wild and domesticated species. They require increasing levels of increasingly potent herbicides, antibiotics, supplemental feeds: mechanical interventions become more frequent and invasive. Increasingly this is being seen as a treadmill, for susceptibility to disease and crop failure are lessened where risks are spread, and complementary 'wild' companion specie systems naturally deplete attacking predatory processes. Such advantages may best be had from intensive management (not to be confused with intensive levels of artificial inputs) which suggest smaller areas for farm units. The essence of the second principle is thus: promotion of biodiversity in farming and forestry methods, and conservation of existing valuable ecology; not as a 'luxury', but for the sake of the *economic* health of farming as a whole.

Thirdly, and finally, at an abstract level, the real people and communities who constitute generations, past and future, are often lost sight of. In human terms, the survival of the human community and the culture which it expresses is equal in importance to the survival of a broad mass of people, and the individuals which make it up. Thus in addition to (i) economic sustainability, which represents the technical efficiency of use of agricultural resources to produce food through time, and (ii) environmental sustainability, representing the maintenance of a diverse genetic capital stock which has the resources to adapt to a variety of external shocks; we propose (iii) the need for demographic sustainability which concerns the optimum size of rural communities and their survival through time. This has the following rationale: green economics is particularly concerned with undervalued resources; in the main, non-renewable energy sources and fragile ecosystems. In the case of rural communities, demographic continuity represents a reservoir of accumulated local knowledge and skill, including social skills and methods of organisation formerly contained in religious activity, but still evident in the vitality of interest in local rural concerns. Under current conditions, for example, knowledge of what can be produced, where and what action to take under specific weather conditions, counts for very little, as chemical or mechanical intervention makes key farming decisions less uncertain. In future it could be much more valuable. So often the agricultural community has been dazzled by the cleverness of a new technology, a machine or genetically engineered plant variety, only later to realise that what they replaced had some value after all, and that usually what was lost was much more costly to replace. It has often been argued that, in the particular circumstances of Wales, its distinct language is the only viable indigenous element of cultural pluralism remaining in the British Isles. The rôle of the agricultural community as the bedrock of that linguistic diversity has been thoroughly investigated (Hughes and Midmore, 1990). The essence of the third principle is thus: concern for the place of people as part of the environment, and recognition of their importance and legitimacy within natural systems.

In the short-term, the future of agriculture in Wales is unlikely to be much influenced by any of these principles, as it is more or less predetermined by the decision taken in May 1992 to reform the CAP (EC, 1992a). On a longer time scale, many questions have been left unanswered, especially in relation to how the finances of the European Union will stand the budgetary strains which the reform agreement imposes, and how a settlement of the GATT Uruguay Round will require changes in the method of agricultural support.

Cereals are the keystone supporting the whole edifice of aid to agriculture. Prices have been extremely high relative to those prevailing on world markets (though to be fair, the latter are also artificially *low* because many other countries, including the United States, interfere with trade and production). This has been achieved by means of levies to keep out imports; when the internal EU price has fallen member states purchase surpluses on behalf of the EU authorities, keep them in storage and eventually provide the subsidies required to effect a sale outside the domestic market. This increasingly expensive policy has caused strains between the member states in the Union, for some believe too much is spent on agricultural support and that more regional aid is required. The voluntary set-aside scheme has not been successful in controlling expenditure, as financial incentives for participation have not attracted a large enough area. Thus under the new arrangements, cereal prices will be reduced over three years to almost (but not quite) world market levels; compensation will be paid to arable farms on the basis of the area under cultivation during a recent reference period, rather than the output which they produce (that is, it will be equivalent to the loss that they would have incurred, and any technical improvements in yield will not increase the payment); but this will depend on voluntary compliance in setting aside at least fifteen per cent of their land. Though these current changes in policy will have the effect of making the dumping of European cereals onto world markets less likely, there are a number of other problems which threaten to wreck at least the budgetary plans for agriculture. Calculations have been made on the basis of no overall cereal yield rise: yet it is virtually impossible, save in the circumstances of a series of disastrous harvests, for yields not to rise in response to this type of scheme. Effort and expertise is concentrated on a smaller area. Indeed it is not outside the range of global experience of this type of scheme for *total* production to rise in response to area constraints on arable production.

The single largest element of the EU's agriculture budget is devoted to cereals, and the consequences of an over-run in this area could be worse for other commodity support programmes (especially the livestock premiums which are currently maintaining the incomes of so many Welsh farms). The budget's growth is linked by Regulation to the growth of the GDP of all twelve member states, so that the resources available are shrinking as the demands on them are increasing. The consequences may be magnified in the medium term if the reform does not — as the Union (alone) argues — meet the terms of the GATT agreement on reform of the world trade system, otherwise known as the Dunkel compromise. This requires a reduction in both the volume of subsidised cereal exports and the value of the payments made, as well as a cut in the value of internal support. More pessimistic commentators envisage set-aside rising to twenty or even thirty per cent of arable land area in order to obtain sufficient cuts in surplus production.

Whilst this may be debatable, the fact that the continued existence of the CAP depends on set-aside at all is a source of serious environmental concern. In the first instance, it involves deliberately wasting a renewable source of food production, land, in order to use non-renewable resources more intensively, and perhaps with more damaging effect to the long term sustainability of the soil on the remaining area; it would surely be far better to use the whole land area less intensively with a lower rate of resource depletion, especially as there will still be some subsidised export and as a result still some import of so-called cereal substitutes for livestock feed. These are, in the main, feedgrains and other staple carbohydrates from countries which have segments of their population suffering from malnutrition; in Europe, they are fed to animals which will in turn be fed to people who for the most part suffer from diseases caused by over-nutrition. This is an irony which would be exquisite if only its consequences were not so bitter for so many.

The fundamental flaw remains in the core of the package of reforms which alter the method of support for agriculture, and until its insidiously pervasive effects are recognised progress towards sustainability in agriculture will be weak and uncertain. Accepting this, there are signs of a positive change in attitude which must be recognised and supported. Some of the consequences of earlier reform proposals, examined in a Welsh context by Midmore (1990, 1992), would have been damaging to the rural economy. In the event, the agreement which will be implemented is likely to have a broadly neutral aggregate economic effect on farming over the three years which the package is due to run. Since the withdrawal of sterling from the European Monetary System, currency depreciation has led to increased returns for commodities linked to prices expressed in ECU.

The reforms continue and consolidate a move away from payments linked to output, to ones linked to area or the number of livestock, removing an imperative to technological yield promotion, but at the same time freezing patterns of land use and adding an additional barrier to the restructuring of farm businesses on less intensive lines. However, perhaps the most appealing shift is usage of funds formerly employed in commodity support (technically, the guarantee section of FEOGA) to an agri-environmental action, concentrating on environmental renovation measures rather than merely conservation. The drawback is that, as a proportion of planned expenditure, the funds available are pitifully small, and the Regulation which implements the agreement is worded loosely, allowing mere gestures to be made. The recently announced Welsh Office scheme (based on Welsh Office, 1993) is disappointing because, as in so many other respects, it merely mirrors the English example when the framework offered a chance to do something really innovative.

Measured against the principles proposed at the outset of this chapter, there seems to be little of any substance in policy initiatives which might shift Welsh agriculture to a more sustainable basis.

There is nothing which will affect the general trends towards more specialisation and dependence on high energy inputs, save perhaps some encouragement to use more cereals as prices are reduced; there may be some discouragement of cereal production in the predominantly livestock-producing areas of Wales, which was previously profitable because of the high transport costs of cereals from the East.

The funding of zonal schemes under the agri-environment programme will certainly be of economic benefit to farmers, as the Minister of Agriculture implied when announcing the recent designation of Environmentally Sensitive Areas, in which farmers can make agreements to receive payments in exchange for managing land in favour of an ecological rather than economic interest. But such schemes are hindered by limited resources and are vulnerable to future reduction in aid before they have discernible impact.

The economic decline of agriculture will probably continue. Apart from milk, competitors for the main Welsh livestock activities are not producers of similar grass-based commodities elsewhere in Britain, but white meats based on intensive industrial systems which use cereal-based feeds which of course will fall in price. On the other hand, prospects for milk are not good either. Though surpluses of milk products are a major problem in the EU, the recent reforms have evaded any sustained effort to deal with this problem. However, changes in the marketing system, with a possibility that producers in more favoured locations will be able to sell directly to milk manufacturers, may reduce the pool price which is the source of stability and security for producers in Wales. As a consequence, more economic decline in rural Wales is likely, as agriculture faces increasingly difficult circumstances. About 300 people who work in agriculture in the hills and uplands of Wales leave each year, as the rural economy, communities and environment bleed to a slow death accompanied, not by the environmental degradation seen elsewhere in rural Britain, but simply by neglect and decay.

It would be a mistake, however, to consider that positive changes come about solely as a result of central determined policy actions, or are necessarily directly proportional in impact to the amount of resources which they consume. The most hopeful signs of renewal in rural Wales come from local initiatives, often from statutory support which is permissive rather than prescriptive, and for the most part based on finance which is both slender in volume and precarious in origin, if it exists at all. The remainder of this chapter examines three such areas of activity as examples of what can be achieved with commitment: action to renovate neglected woodlands on farms; organic farming; and rural development schemes, based on community involvement, to promote economic change with minimum environmental impact.

Farm Forestry

Farm forestry is being promoted as an alternative to agricultural land use, by means of grant aid for planting and management. This is intended to achieve two ends at once; land carrying trees cannot easily be switched back into agricultural production, and with Britain as a whole highly dependent on the import of timber, with forecast rises in demand for wood and wood products, planting now will eventually provide an alternative income source for farmers as the crop is harvested. Grants are increased for better quality land, and for plantations which are predominantly of broad-leaf species, in the hope that they will provide greater environmental benefit.

However, what makes sense at a national level does not necessarily translate into a rational policy at the level of the local rural economy. Even though grants are available to compensate for the poor returns to forestry over its production cycle, putting land under trees still involves farmers in considerable losses of income. In the uplands of Wales, there is already too much forestry: a visually apparent fact to anyone familiar with the area. More importantly, what forestry does exist is of the wrong type. A predominance of uniform age softwood plantations, in addition to environmental concerns expressed above, does little to promote local economic activity; its low value necessitates least-cost harvesting and processing: clear-felling, and haulage over long distances for processing in capital-intensive plants.

In addition to plantation forestry there is a considerably greater area of semi-natural woodland, which, at least until the end of the last century, was managed as an integrated part of the rural economy. To a large extent, selective felling of trees and natural regeneration preserved species diversity and associated environmental benefits. But most of the woodland of this type, which is predominantly on farms, has fallen into disuse and decay; many of the trees are over-mature, others have unintentionally grown up from stools left from previous felling, and undergrazing now prevents natural regeneration. The most recent Agricultural Census shows that there are 36,463 hectares of woodland on farms in Wales: a considerable proportion of this will be semi-natural, and possibly ancient in origin. One of the major findings of a recent study of pluriactivity (i.e. income generation from multiple sources) on farms in Wales was that renovation of neglected woodlands has considerably greater linkage with the local rural economy than plantation forestry. Depending on circumstances, between 40 and 120 per cent more income is generated by the former, and between 3.5 and 6 times as much employment (Bateman *et al*, 1993, p V-22).

It has been the aim of the organisation *Coed Cymru* to promote greater utilisation of this resource to provide a greater degree of integration with the rest of the local rural economy, based on higher added-value, and use in other rural industries, of the higher quality timber that can be produced. This, together with a production cycle based on continuous rather than intermittent output, is the key which can transform the otherwise gloomy economic and environmental characteristics of forestry.

The first aim, because of the loss of habitat which is presently occurring, is to bring existing farm woodlands back into productive management. Farmers themselves can usually provide the labour for this, because woodland management operations can be done at a slack time of year. Adequate fencing is needed to exclude livestock (which, due to the limited quality and availability of the grass under trees, does not usually have a great impact on the farm's stock carrying capacity) and some selective felling is needed to restart the process of regeneration — perhaps assisting nature by planting new trees consistent with the overall species mix. Much of the timber extracted will be of low initial quality, though a proportion is suitable for processing. Because of the small-scale nature of the operation, most of the farmers have the kind of equipment necessary, in the form of tractors, trailers and chainsaws. The initial rôle of *Coed Cymru* is therefore to assist in management planning, providing the knowledge and skills necessary to carry out the operations for optimum economic and environmental benefit. In the first four years of its existence, the organisation assisted in bringing an area of 3,500 hectares (8,600 acres) into management (*Coed Cymru*, 1988, 1990). In time, once the practice of woodland management becomes an established part of diversified farm businesses, there will be scope for incremental extensions of the existing semi-natural woodland area on farms.

The second aim is to revive demand in local markets in order to absorb the increased supplies of locally produced hardwood. There is a need to improve information about the quality of the new source of fuel, fencing and other construction material. To a large extent the market is saturated by cheaper, mass-produced imports, though the key here is the fact that, because of new 'intermediate' tractor-driven technology, local timber can provide some products of a far higher quality. Chestnut fencing stakes, for example, require no treatment before use (softwood substitutes are poorly treated and thus do not last as long); hardwood planking materials and other construction products are becoming increasingly available and are now identified as 'locally produced'. Firewood is now often advertised as coming from sustainably managed woodland, appealing to a small, but growing, distinctive and influential market.

The major problem is in providing the impetus to start off this process. Output from initial harvesting operations is mostly of poor quality and until recently has been sold for pulping. This used to provide a return which, together with some grant aid for management, has been reasonable enough to justify the costs involved in restoring fencing, laying tracks in woods to aid extraction, and contractors' costs where necessary. Since the considerable price reduction for pulping timber, it has become much more difficult to persuade farmers to undertake this necessary environmental work: there is a desperate need for an alternative which could provide comparable returns. One major possibility, which demonstrates potential links between activities at a local level, is to use such wood for combined heat and power projects based on bio-fuels. There exists a well-developed Scandinavian technology for chipping and utilising wood in a highly energy efficient way, at a cost which, when the substantial proportion accounted for by transport is included, is below the cost of oil in rural areas. There is an objection that waste wood supplies will decline in volume once the effect of re-established management has improved the quality of timber output from semi-natural areas, allowing its utilisation for fencing, construction and furniture making. This could be offset by re-establishing coppice woodlands specifically for the purpose of energy cropping. From the point of view of supporting a wide range of species, coppicing as a subsidiary part of the overall management of woodland areas would promote a further habitat layer.

Nevertheless, because the area of semi-natural ancient woodlands which exists is finite, judicious planting, especially where it extends adjacent to existing areas, can improve the quality of the environmental resource. In addition, there is the possibility of a shortage of softwood in the early decades of the coming century, and if that is to be met partly from domestic resources, more conifer planting will be needed. Ecological arguments for conservation and management are well-established, but it can now be demonstrated that an equally powerful economic argument exists.

Organic farming

Organic farming has had a high profile in recent years, but the number of organic farms remains very small at around one hundred, a fraction of one per cent of the farms and land area in Wales. The Welsh organic farms are characteristically smaller than average, with a greater reliance on horticulture and processing activities than their conventional counterparts. This is in part a reflection of many of the adopters of organic farming in the late 1970s and early 1980s, with an emphasis on self-sufficiency small-holding by former (and mainly English) urban dwellers. Some have successfully established viable businesses and integrated with the local community, but there is also now evidence of increased business from indigenous, established farmers, who form the majority of current adopters of organic farming methods.

Despite its current small scale, organic farming continues to offer significant environmental and social benefits in terms of environmental protection, conservation of non-renewable resources, improved food quality, reduction in output of surplus products, rural employment and the re-orientation of agriculture towards areas of market demand. Many governments in Western and Central Europe have recognised and responded to these potential benefits by encouraging farmers to adopt organic farming practices, either directly through financial incentives or indirectly through support for research, extension and marketing initiatives. Even without government support, the organic sector throughout Europe is expanding rapidly and is seen by an increasing number of mainstream commentators to have considerable potential. In the UK, thirty-eight per cent of the 26,000 farmers who responded to a 1991 postal questionnaire, stated that they would consider, or were considering, organic production on all or part of their land in future (NatWest, 1992). In Wales the proportion was even higher, at forty-five per cent. It is clear that there is considerable latent interest among conventional farmers which is not yet reflected in the numbers using organic methods.

The debate on the potential rôle of organic farming has been confused by some significant misconceptions, not least the frequently used definition of organic farming as farming without artificial fertilisers and pesticides. Although non-use of most agrochemicals is an important characteristic of organic farming, the definition fails to take account of the environmental, social and animal welfare objectives of organic farming which underpin specific production practices. A more appropriate definition would be that organic producers seek to create integrated, sustainable agricultural systems by relying primarily on farm-derived, renewable resources as well as ecological interactions and biological processes for crop, livestock and human nutrition and protection from pests and diseases. The term 'sustainable' is used in a wider sense, to encompass not just conservation of non-renewable resources (soil, energy, minerals) but also issues of environmental and social sustainability. The term 'organic' is best thought of as referring not to the type of fertilisers used, but to the concept of the farm as an organism, in which all the component parts — the soil, minerals, organic matter, micro-organisms, insects, plants, animals and humans — interact to create a coherent whole. In many European countries, organic farming is known as ecological agriculture, reflecting this reliance on ecosystem management rather than external inputs, chemical or otherwise.

A detailed description of the principles and practices of organic farming in the United Kingdom can be found in Lampkin (1990). Formal guidelines are laid down in the standard documents of the International Federation of Organic Agriculture Movements (IFOAM, 1992), the Soil Association (SA, 1992) and the UK Register of Organic Food Standards (UKROFS, 1992). These guidelines are reinforced by legislation in the European Union (EC, 1991) and the United States (US., 1990) and are the subject of proposals for international guidelines (FAO, 1991).

Although much has been made of food quality issues and the potential advantages of organic farming in this respect, the major contribution which organic systems offer is probably in terms of their environmental impact. A number of reports in the UK (e.g. Arden-Clarke, 1988a; Arden Clarke, 1988b; NCC, 1990; Redman, 1992) and abroad (e.g. Koening, Sunkel et al., 1989) provide significant support for the case that organic farming can contribute to soil, flora and fauna conservation and to a general reduction in pollution from agricultural sources. This potential has been recognised by a number of governments, notably Austria, Denmark, Sweden and Germany and more recently by the European Union (EC, 1992b).

Organic farming also offers some rural employment benefits, through higher labour use on more diversified farms, and through the impact of associated processing and marketing initiatives. Examples of these include a number of farmhouse cheese makers and meat processors in Dyfed and Powys, as well as the major organic packing and processing companies such as Organic Farm Foods (Wales) and Welsh Organic Foods in Lampeter, and Rachel's Dairy in Aberystwyth. We have estimated that the employment benefits of organic farming in Wales outweigh the losses associated with reduced input purchases, thus providing higher overall employment levels, and an increased return to labour, both farm family and hired, on organic farms in Wales (Bateman *et al.*, 1993; Lampkin and Bateman, 1993).

Despite these advantages, farmers are still reluctant to convert because of the perceived high costs of doing so, and the risks involved, even though premium markets for organically produced food are now making it possible for (full-time) organic producers to earn similar incomes to their conventional counterparts (Lampkin, 1993a; Lampkin and Bateman, 1993). This lack of confidence on the part of conventional farmers is not surprising, given decades of antagonism to the concept of organic farming and the distribution of sometimes inaccurate and misleading information by extension agencies; the vested interests of the agrochemical industry; and the lack of access to sound information and advice on the subject.

This situation is beginning to change, in part because of the general recognition of the problems associated with intensive, conventional production methods, but also because, as the organic sector grows, more farmers are having contact with viable, working examples of organic farms in their locality. The implicit recognition given to organic farming by the involvement of major food companies in the market for organic food, and by the development of policies to support organic farming by governments around the world, is also providing a significant boost to the credibility of the organic approach.

As a consequence, there is now evidence from Austria, Germany and the Scandinavian countries that, given appropriate support, organic farming can break out of the 'fraction of one per cent' agricultural ghetto to become a realistic, mainstream agricultural alternative. In 1992 alone, two per cent of former East German farmland was converted to organic production, and in one state, Mecklenburg-Vorpommern, eight per cent of farms and five per cent of farmland was converted (Lampkin, 1993b). Germany as a whole has seen the number of organic farms increase from 3,000 to over 12,500 in the period 1989 to 1993, with the area of organically managed land increasing from under 50,000 to nearly 400,000 hectares. In Austria, the number of organic farms has increased from under 2,000 to nearly 9,000 in the same period.

Growth in the UK (and in Wales) has been much slower, with the number of farms increasing from 600 to 800 since 1989, although the land area has increased from 15,000 to 35,000 hectares, reflecting the larger size of farms now converting to organic production. The key difference has been government inaction, in terms of significant support for organic farming research, education, training, advice, market development and financial support for conversion. The recently announced Welsh Office scheme to support conversion to organic farming (Welsh Office, 1993) risks perpetuating this situation, through very low payment levels, particularly in less favoured areas, and through restrictions on the number of farms, and the land area, which will be supported. The proposals do nothing to counteract the effects of the CAP reform, which, through the introduction of quotas and other restrictions on entitlement to livestock and arable aid payments, introduces a new barrier to the restructuring of farm business which conversion to organic farming entails, and exacerbates the financial difficulties associated with the conversion period. At the same time, no proposals have been put forward to improve the training and advisory services available to farmers converting to organic production, an essential co-requisite to financial support to ensure that the adverse financial aspects of conversion are minimised and that the environmental and other benefits which are sought will in fact be achieved.

Bottom-up Community Development

One of the most important lessons which has been learned in poor rural areas of developing countries is that unless the aid efforts which they receive are co-ordinated, possibilities of duplication, or even conflict between efforts, emerge. The greater the number of directions from which aid comes, the higher the probability of failure becomes. It is therefore not surprising that in Wales, with so many statutory bodies having (hierarchically arranged) responsibility for so many aspects of rural economic, social and environmental affairs, recipients of their attention at local level have become somewhat sceptical. Some have become so sceptical that they have organised themselves into community development organisations which take on the task of co-ordination of the many sectorally-based forms of aid which are available. Those which have been successful have, in the main, relied on the efforts of a single individual around whose inspiration an organisation has been built, though of course it would be better (and this is the eventual aim) if communities as a whole possessed the necessary skills which could be utilised to help this process.

The economic problem, baldly stated, is one of choice between different uses for the limited range of resources which the country-side has to offer. If rural communities need to exchange goods and services derived from that resource base, the choice needs to be made prudently in order to derive maximum benefit in relation to the least possible disturbance, in terms of the overall quality of life, rather than just the number of new jobs or enhancement of money incomes. Decisions made by an economic élite will rarely achieve such a balance, unless informed and guided by what people themselves actually want.

For example, tourism is often cited as the economic activity which has most to offer rural areas. However, there are important questions about the ability of the rural resource to adequately absorb any extra volume of tourist activity. Characteristics of country holidays sought by customers include tranquillity, particularly freedom from congestion, and a clean environment. As any increase in tourist activity in rural areas is most likely to be car-based, negative feed-back effects may quickly become evident. But more seriously, very often a greater proportion of local people do not benefit from the economic activity itself whilst suffering from all its costs. Therefore new activity needs to be discussed widely, and to be implemented slowly so that any unwanted impacts can be foreseen and avoided; the effect of tourism developments within a rural locality can be quite major, even though to an outsider their scale may seem trivial. Schemes which disperse tourist activity, linking it to dispersed expenditure so that a wide range of businesses benefit, are likely to have a higher economic/environmental impact ratio. For example, walking holidays, based on a network of footpaths, scenic and archaeological attractions, and linked to a corresponding network of farmhouse accommodation, could have the desired economic effect with almost no disruptive impact. The key is organisation, especially between people and their small rural businesses.

The EU's LEADER (links between action for the development of rural economies) project has encouraged and assisted schemes which incorporate a number of features which stimulate local community action of this kind. Funds, though, are limited; greater sums spread over a wider area are needed for effective action. Often government regulation militates against the creation of links between communities, the economic and environmental sphere. An example is the close regulation of local government finances: obliged to purchase as economically as possible, opportunities for purchasing locally produced hardwoods for countryside furniture or construction are limited on grounds of cost. Yet if there were freedom to take account of environmental and social benefit, greater improvements in the quality of life would result: as it is, even the economic benefit in terms of longer lasting materials and creation of worthwhile employment, are sacrificed in favour of short-term cost reduction. The principle, worth reiterating, is that decisions should be taken as close to the point of their impact as possible. But because this is dependent on a set of skills which have fallen into disuse through lack of exercise, there is a need for gradual re-education on a community basis. Changes which come about as a result of a 'bottom-up' approach to rural development cannot be wrought rapidly, but the effects can be longer-lasting, and gain more social acceptance, than those made by conventional processes.

Conclusion

The future for Welsh agriculture, and its rural, social and environmental context, is bleak if current policies are not altered. The so-called CAP reform of 1992 will at best do little to control surplus production and budgetary costs, and at worst has the potential to cause serious social and environmental damage. The supplementary measures contained in the agri-environment programme may provide some environmental benefits in small areas, but the funds available are severely restricted, particularly when placed in the context of the main livestock and arable aid schemes.

A new, more fundamental review of agricultural policy is urgently required. We have identified a number of principles which we believe should form the basis for this change in direction:

- Agriculture should be seen as an integral part of the rural economy, alongside forestry, tourism and other rural activities. This requires an integrated approach to policy development.
- The maintenance and *enhancement* of social, cultural and environmental quality should become key goals of rural policy, alongside traditional economic objectives.
- There should be a direct and corresponding transfer of funds away from agricultural commodity support to payment for environmental enhancement, and improvements to the quality of rural social and economic life.
- Rural policy should be based on the principle of bottom-up, local, community and individual action, providing opportunities and support for genuine involvement and innovation by those who are intended to benefit.

We have tried to indicate some initiatives, such as farm forestry, organic farming, and community involvement as in the south Pembrokeshire LEADER programme, where elements of this new, integrated approach to rural policy are beginning to evolve. But in all these areas, progress is hindered by the same lack of any holistic vision which prevents the more fundamental reform of agricultural and rural policy which we believe is sorely needed. It remains an open question how long it will take before serious reform, with genuine concern for the environmental and social conditions of rural areas, reaches the top of the agenda for those in government, and elsewhere, who are in a position to bring about the radical changes which are required.

References

Arden-Clarke, C. (1988a). *The environmental effects of conventional and organic/biological farming systems. I. Impact on the soil.* Research Reports, RR-16. Political Ecology Research Group; Oxford.

Arden-Clarke, C. (1988b). *The environmental effects of conventional and organic/biological farming systems. II. Impacts on the crop ecosystem, wildlife and its habitats.* Research Reports, RR-17. Political Ecology Research Group; Oxford.

Bateman, D.I., G.O. Hughes, P. Midmore, N.H. Lampkin and C.S. Ray

(1993). *Pluriactivity and the Rural Economy in the Less Favoured Areas of Wales*. Report to the ESRC Department of Economics and Agricultural Economics, University of Wales; Aberystwyth.

Coed Cymru, (1988). *The First Two Years*. Coed Cymru; Newtown.

Coed Cymru, (1990). *Two Year Report September 1988 - August 1990*. Coed Cymru; Newtown.

Department of the Environment (1990). *This Common Inheritance: Britain's environmental strategy*. Command Paper 1200. HMSO; London.

EC (1991). Council Regulation (EEC) No 2092/91 of 24 June 1991 on organic production of agricultural products and indications referring thereto on agricultural products and foodstuffs. *Official Journal of the European Communities*. 91 (L198):1-15.

EC (1992a). Regulation (EEC) No 1765/92 establishing a support scheme for producers of certain arable crops. *Official Journal of the European Communities*. L181(2/7/92):12.

EC (1992b). Council Regulation (EEC) No 2078/92 on agricultural production methods compatible with the requirements of the protection of the environment and the maintenance of the countryside. *Official Journal of the European Communities*. L215 (30/7/92):85-90.

FAO. (1991). *Draft guidelines for production, processing, labelling and marketing of organic/bio-dynamic foods*. Codex Alimentarius Commission, Food and Agriculture Organisation: Rome.

Hughes, G.O. and P. Midmore (1990). 'Agrarian Change and Rural Society: a Regional Case-Study Approach'. Paper presented at the XIVth Congress of the European Society for Rural Sociology, Giessen, July 1990.

IFOAM. (1992). *Basic Standards of Organic Agriculture*. International Federation of Organic Agriculture Movements; Tholey-Theley, Germany.

Koenig, W., R. Sunkel, U. Necker, R. Wolff-Straub, S. Ingrisch, U. Wasner and E. Glueck. (1989). *Alternativer und konventioneller Landbau — Vergleichsuntersuchungen von Ackerflaechen auf Loessstandorten im Rheinland*. Schriftenreihe der Landesanstalt fuer Oekologie, Landschaftsentwicklung und Forstplanung Nordrhein-Westfalen, Landwirtschaftsverlag; Muenster-Hiltrup.

Lampkin, N.H. (1990). *Organic Farming*. Farming Press; Ipswich.

Lampkin, N.H. (1993a). *The economic implications of conversion from conventional to organic farming systems*. PhD Thesis. Department of Economics and Agricultural Economics, University of Wales; Aberystwyth.

Lampkin, N.H. (1993b). 'The impact of governmental financial assistance on the adoption of organic farming in Germany'. Discussion Paper Series 93/2. Centre for Organic Husbandry and Agroecology, University of Wales; Aberystwyth.

Midmore, P. (1990). *The Agricultural Crisis and West Wales*. Dyfed County

Council; Carmarthen.

Midmore, P. (1992). 'The MacSharry Proposals and the Welsh Rural Economy'. *Welsh Economic Review*, 4(2), 42:49.

NatWest. (1992). *National Farm Survey*. National Westminster Bank; Coventry.

NCC. (1990). *Nature conservation and agricultural change*. Focus on Nature Conservation, 25. Nature Conservancy Council; Peterborough.

Redman, M. (1992). *Organic farming and the countryside*. British Organic Farmers; Bristol.

SA (1992). *Standards for Organic Food and Farming*. Soil Association Organic Marketing Co. Ltd.; Bristol.

UKROFS. (1992). *UKROFS Standards for Organic Food Production*. UK Register of Organic Food Standards, Food From Britain; London.

US (1990). *Organic Foods Production Act of 1990*. United States Senate Committee on Agriculture, Nutrition and Forestry; Washington D.C.

Welsh Office (1993). *Agriculture and Wales' Environment*. Welsh Office Agriculture Department; Cardiff.

World Commission on Environment and Development (1989). *Our Common Future*. Oxford University Press; Oxford.

Robert Minhinnick

Urban Wales: the Environment of the Majority

Behind Port Talbot looms a mountain named Mynydd Emroch. This is a typical Welsh eminence, cropped by sheep, crowned with a television mast, and once subject to a contentious planning proposal for a seven turbine wind-farm. In fine weather it is a salutary experience to scramble up its slopes and gaze down over the coastal plain of West Glamorgan. For despite the media apparatus on Emroch, when at its summit, the climber is part of rural Wales. To the north for several miles there is nothing but farmsteads, a maze of *ffriddoedd* and streams, vast acreages of new forestry and scraps of older woodland. But, to the south, and neck-craningly to the west and east, is one of the most intensively industrialised urban environments of this country, fifty years old and already displaying signs of exhaustion.

Urban Wales, created by iron two hundred years ago, developed by the winning and trading of coal, slate, then tin-plate, steel, chemicals, and the capital's foundries of bureaucracy, is the environment of the majority. It is true that twenty per cent of the country is now National Park. There are nearly nine hundred Sites of Special Scientific Interest and an increasing number of officially-acknowledged areas of environmental sensitivity and outstanding natural beauty. There also exist landscapes without habitation and other places where people are outnumbered by some of the thirteen million Welsh sheep at a ratio of hundreds to one. But any examination of an environment must include how its population

135

relates to it, for good or ill. Without the activities of its people, Wales would be unnamed, inhospitable and inexplicable. The tragedy is that certain of those activities have left it, in part, seriously damaged.

Fifty years ago the plain below Mynydd Emroch consisted of marshes, pools, sea-meadows and orchid-rich duneland. It was farmed, but not intensively. The villages of Margam, Taibach and Baglan, the mini-conurbation which we know today as Port Talbot, impinged on the area with their traffic and commerce, but not too destructively.

Looking back, it is tempting, but inaccurate, to view the developments of the time as almost 'sustainable'. Sustainability, of course, is a term that has now been imbued with a totemic modern significance. Irony of ironies, it is currently the talismanic word of both the environmental movement and twenty-first century-hungry big business. Like most such keywords, its meaning has never been satisfactorily defined. Thus 'sustainability' has swelled into vacuity, and engendered its own cumulus of unmeaning. Nevertheless, when I speak to older inhabitants of the Port Talbot area today, I hear the plain described in idyllic, even romantic terms, which provides an illuminating example of how much the urban Welsh are already alienated from their own, predominantly rural country, the *morfa* that was, the hillsides beyond Emroch that remain.

To the east lies the five-miles-long British Steel plant, fringed with fire, as smoky and complex as a blitzed city. Straight ahead are the red brick warrens and treeless avenues of the 'good-idea-at-the-time' Sandfields estate, whilst to the west is BP Baglan Bay, architecturally and sometimes literally breath-taking, a conglomeration of mauves and silvers shimmering in the dusk, brutal in broad daylight, a halo of flame pulsing at its enormous gas-venting chimney. Spielberg's UFO, if it had landed on what used to be the Baglan marshes, could not have made a more extraordinary impact on the environment. And in front of these monuments of urban Wales snakes the M4, ever-widening, ever-snarled in its Port Talbot-Briton Ferry incarnation, and now climbing on a series of concrete monoliths over the River Neath.

This is a landscape with the drama of Snowdonia, the eeriness of the Welsh 'empty quarter' (the north Ceredigion-Merionnydd-

Maldwyn high ground), and a great deal more danger. Seen from the hillside, there is an initially satisfying geometry to the development, an orderliness which the olive-green slopes behind cannot achieve. But a resort to binoculars subverts the pleasure. The dunes beyond the 'heavy end' of the steelworks have been obliterated and replaced with iridescent tumuli of flux, slag and ash. The neighbouring Corsican pine-wood with its unusual helleborines has been undermined and, in places, levelled, as a result of the steelworks' appetite for sand. If the 'right to pollute' is a form of anarchy, then here is one place in Wales where human violence puts into context the unpitying law of the natural world.

If such regrettable yet unavoidable (as many would say) atrocities were perpetuated only against the topography and its plant-life, urban Wales would be a happier place. Yet the facts illustrate that equally grievous harm has been done to the very people who have helped create and sustain the municipal environments of this country. The Welsh are primarily a working-class people, and the health of our working-classes has been so damaged by the environmental consequences of urbanisation, that our respiratory and heart disease rates are amongst the worst in the world, our incidence of cancer is shocking, and our physical fitness, corroded in the last generation by the revolution in junk-food — or urban food as it might be termed — is poor. Rickets and tuberculosis might be part of the past (although TB is making an ominous comeback) but the consequences of obesity and asthma, the twin working-class plagues of late twentieth century Wales, are everywhere.

Port Talbot, if we might remain on the slopes of Mynydd Emroch a while longer, provides evidence for much of this. Because of the quantities of muck which its industry emits into the atmosphere, Port Talbot has been fairly, if controversially, described as the dirtiest town in Wales. (An annual eighty tons of dust per square mile have been known to fall in some areas). Four pressure groups, comprising ordinary members of the community, have consistently throughout the last decade drawn attention to the threats posed by air pollution to human health. Their chief obstacle, as elsewhere in Wales, has been an entrenched political establishment, the members of which have often found their own employment with the polluters. This hegemony continues to exist in ignorance and suspicion of environmental issues, whilst feeling itself burdened with the knowledge that without the massive rents charged to local industry, the borough would be an even more ramshackle area than it is today.

It is difficult to over-estimate the problems that are created in parts of Wales by the belief of certain political dynasties that power is invested in them naturally and eternally. Over the generations a gulf of cynicism and apathy has widened between the actual power-bearers and their notional masters — the public. And it is in environmental terms that this chasm is usually most visible.

For Wales is loud with the usually unheard voices of protest, raised against particular threats stemming from the urban environment — but threats which will be unfamiliar to most of the population. However these urban environmentalists conduct themselves, whether in action groups, coalitions or through individual action, their profile remains low. For theirs are not the great environmental causes of rural Wales, championed by the English middle-classes, imperious poets and the Sunday broadsheets. These Welsh people have not joined in the emblematic campaigns to prevent the pipeline scarring Cwm Dyli in Snowdonia, against the quarrying of the 'ecological cathedral' of Carmel Woods in Dyfed, against jet-skis, sewage-pumping and oil and gas exploration in Cardigan Bay.

But neither are theirs the self-interested and ineffective meddlings of which they are sometimes accused. Their mundane battles concern plans to build a toxic-waste processing plant in the middle of Newport, the emissions from chemical and smelting works in Clwyd and Mid Glamorgan, the extension of an opencast mine to within yards of a housing estate, the deadly spore of an incineration plant in a Gwent valley, and the legacy of old industrial contamination on trading-estate sites in Dyfed that has seen even cockroaches, predicted to survive a nuclear winter, dropping dead from cadmium poisoning.

Urban Wales is therefore quite capable of threatening the life-quality of its citizens by the same means with which it provides a living and lifestyle. But the urban environment is itself constantly changing, and is perceived by many to be under threat. It is as natural for a town-dweller to mourn, for example, the dereliction of the Victorian pier at Colwyn Bay, as others might protest at the uprooting of hedgerows. Perhaps the most extreme example of such feeling is the creation of a conservation group in Merthyr Tydfil, dedicated to the protection of an ancient iron and slag tip. This mound, the group claims, is part of the town's heritage, indeed one of the few last traces of its industrial heyday that has not been swept away in the urban regeneration of Merthyr, which has seen Georgetown wiped out, The Triangle dispatched to the Welsh Folk Museum, and the tiny terrace where Joseph Parry flourished, bizarrely surrounded by a new 'Brookside'-like series of 'closes'.

And yet it is difficult to imagine the great council estates of Merthyr Tydfil, "that armpit of a town" as it was once described, attracting such devotion. But there, in Galon Uchaf (or 'Hatchet Land' as some of the denizens know it) and the equally-desertified Gurnos, is Welsh urban architecture, and perhaps Welsh urban life, at its most brutally functional. Nevertheless, it is always chastening to discover in Merthyr that greetings are still exchanged between strangers, and that there is enough outward friendliness on the streets to engender suspicion that your own community's values, based now largely on the consumer paranoia of Neighbourhood Watch, might require evaluation.

But sentimentality is no ally in Galon Uchaf. The elementary gridiron design of the estate soon becomes tedious. Worse is the obvious lack of interest from the councillors who approved the estate, for its streets are titled 'First Avenue', 'Second Avenue' all the way up to the imaginative heights of 'Eleventh Avenue'.

Perhaps regretting such pedestrianism, as compensation the streets of Gurnos are named after every flower and tree in the gardener's almanac. Yet a combination of the local canine mafia, terrorist sheep and the wind that shaves much of mid Wales to a damp desert of khaki grass, ensures that there are few opportunities for local flora to flourish. More obvious here are the great white blooms of the satellite dishes. Like most of urban Wales, these estates have their fair share of technological acne. But satellite snobbery renders many of us hypocrites. It is easy to sneer at dishes whilst forgetting the ugly metal numerals of television aerials sprouting from our own chimneys. Nevertheless, satellite systems are powerful symbols of our time. They hint at domestic introspection and the growth of global media appetite at the expense of local curiosity and community concern. In this respect, urban Wales is as badly afflicted as anywhere.

Merthyr, the valleys of South Wales, urban Clwyd and old industrial Gwynedd are noticeable for the absence of national environmental pressure groups. Neither Friends of the Earth, the Civic Trust, nor any of the conservation bodies from the political spectrum in between, find much favour. Part of the reason is that these organisations are perceived as uninterested in the problems of urban Wales. This is undoubtedly true. Nobody joins the Campaign for the Protection of Rural Wales, the Royal Society for Nature Conservation or applies for a job with the Countryside Council for Wales with the idea of campaigning against the tipping of hospital rubbish in Dowlais or for the removal of spoil heaps from Blaenau Ffestiniog.

This latter town, in fact, boasts the most dramatic industrial scars in Wales. The high tips of slate scree and other quarrying waste that dominate the area are as impressive in their own way as many of the untouched summits nearby. Slate created a strong urban Welsh-speaking culture that persists today, but a culture that valued the social above the natural environment. There was nothing unusual about that, and because of the contribution of the slate industry to the strength of the Welsh language, it would be futile to pursue this point. The irony today is that old slate towns such as Bethesda have as high a proportion of condemned or inadequate housing as anywhere in Wales. And slate villages such as Corris only survive (if it can be said that they 'survive' at all) by turning the industrial pollution of their employment into tourist-bait.

But in the South, and the valleys especially, the reasons for lack of environmental interest can be allied to a wider absence of significant community political action. Radicalism has been replaced with torpor, and the nursing ground of activists is now scorched earth. It is a difficult business finding the reasons for this, but the decline of community-based industries — the closure of over two hundred coal-mines since nationalisation, for example — must be a contributing factor.

In a decade — the eighties — that saw a world-wide explosion of environmental concern and lobbying — urban Wales remained largely mute on the great issues of the day. There were inevitably some exceptions. In the 1983 General Election, the mining constituency of Ogmore awarded the Green (then Ecology) Party its second highest vote in England and Wales. But for the most part, what action occurred never possessed as its bedrock any ideas gleaned from green philosophy or spirituality; it simply concentrated on minimising the impact of local industry on human health by improved technological processes. Technology itself, the imperative of economic growth, and the concept of man as an industrial servant, were never questioned. Urban Wales, had, after all, been created by faith in these principles. And if valley radicals — whether Labour, Communist or nationalist — railed against the tyranny of industry, an all-round environmentalism was never remotely part of the creed or fighting strategy.

Because of the geography of the valleys, there seems little chance that the traditional architectural style — predominantly long greystone terraces, with doors and lintels painted in Italianate colours — will be replaced. Chapels and Institutes might close and be turned into video-parlours or gymnasiums where youngsters learn oriental martial arts, but the actual shape and identity of the settlements are secure — despite an ageing population, little employment, and the one-way tickets sought by the ambitious and the talented. To outsiders, however, the valleys might appear less a series of villages that bleed into one another than a vast inner-city of 800,000 people, about which are scattered some (by U.K. standards) spectacularly run down and dilapidated areas.

Lowland urban Wales, however, is more easily blurred, rethought and rebuilt. Nowhere is there more proof of this than in what has become known as Cardiff Bay.

This is the biggest city 'regeneration' scheme ever to be undertaken in Wales, concentrating on the Butetown area of the capital, but profoundly affecting almost the entire south of Cardiff. Although the minor grandeur of Mount Stuart Square remains, this area is now unrecognisable from a decade ago. And greater changes are imminent, most prominently the creation of a 200 acre city lagoon, achieved by building a barrage across the mouths of the Taff and Ely rivers. That the last ghosts of Tiger Bay are banished by the development is a necessary act. Wales is a country haunted by its own exhausted mythologies, and it was impossible to preserve the colourful dereliction of the Docks simply because of their folkloric significance.

But constructing the barrage is a completely different matter. In short, it is one of the greatest acts of environmental vandalism to take place in Wales since the war, and its consequences will be felt for years. The wish of Cardiff Bay Development Corporation is to present an inner-city waterfront environment to incoming house-holders and businesses. But this means destroying the tidal flushing system of the bay, the natural cleansing mechanism that is able to dispose of some of the millions of gallons of sewage and industrial waste that are pumped into it every day. Not for nothing have estuaries and river-mouths have been described as the 'kidneys' of the coastline. The CBDC aim is to cosmeticise nature. The glistening shoals of mud, exposed at low tide, providing feeding-grounds of international importance for wading birds, are an embarrassment in a new city environment of pastel-shaded marina flatlets, high-tech studios and administration's atria.

As an acknowledgement of the pollution problem, most water-contact sports are to be forbidden in the newly created lagoon, while special teams of workers will be employed to remove the build-up of putrescent detritus and any algal growth behind the barrage. Campaigners have highlighted the health threats that the increased damp created by the barrage will bring to areas of Cardiff, and also the hot weather dangers of allowing the build-up of a reeking moraine of river-bourne refuse behind the dam.

Yet the concept of a barrage has always had too many political reputations dependent on its success to be seriously endangered. In environmental terms, it was always destructive and unnecessary, but in the reconstruction of Cardiff, environmental considerations have been granted little priority. Various MPs have argued that too much concentration of wealth in the capital will damage industrial enterprise in the valleys. Despite this, the impression created by the Cardiff Bay public relations machine is that objectors using arguments based on the quality of the urban environment have been 'little people' foolishly attempting to obstruct inevitable progress. In the 'new' capital of the 'Cardiff International Arena' and Atlantic Wharf, there is little space for renewal on a human scale.

In fact, for the proposed £170 million that the barrage will cost, Cardiff could have built its own light rail system, which would have been a godsend for those who must travel through the city each day. This in turn would have diminished the need for some of the new roads which the local planners intend to drive through countryside around the city.

Yet organisations such as the RSPB which have opposed the barrage on the grounds that it would displace significant populations of wading and shore-feeding birds, have found that lobbying exercises for dunlin and redshank attract only specialised support. The Welsh environmental movement must learn a lesson from this. Until green organisations can illustrate how the man-made environment — and public health — can also be threatened by foolishly grandiose and falsely 'prestigious' developments, then arguments based purely on wildlife will have minor appeal — at least in a predominantly working-class country such as Wales.

Failure to embrace the major urban issues of the day — transport, road-building, air pollution and the sweeping away of small-scale, sometimes run-down city areas in favour of multi-national funded projects for the leisure consumer — will prove that the Welsh environmental movement is simply inadequate for the tasks confronting it. The movement will appear content to remain the preserve of non-committal scientists, quangos for the comfortably off with time on their hands, and weekend drystone wall-builders and salvagers of frog spawn. In short, it will have chosen marginality.

That is why it has been pleasing in the early nineties to note increased public lobbying in urban Wales on the quality of drinking water, and especially lead pollution caused by old plumbing and street-piping. Indeed, for a variety of reasons, inner-city areas and outer suburbs of Cardiff, such as Cathays, Docklands, Llandaff, and Whitchurch have the worst lead-polluted drinking water in Wales. It must be noted here that when the water leaves the Dŵr Cymru Welsh Water treatment works, this pollution is not present, and that the problem lies in our inheritance of old pipework. Nevertheless, the company's refusal to target those areas it knows possess high levels — particularly schools and hospitals — is disappointing and must be changed.

But however necessary such work, it remains 'single issue' campaigning. It is more difficult to point out successful initiatives of those working on a wider urban front. Indeed, there are those who state that the battle to protect a distinctively Welsh urban

environment is already lost. UK and American commercial con-
glomerates now own many Welsh high streets. The same proprie-
torial signatures dominate Oxford Street, whether in London or
Swansea. The major shopping thoroughfare of Wales — Queen
Street, Cardiff — might be anywhere in the UK, despite the cos-
metic dab of a few bilingual signposts.

These processes of enforced uniformity and urban anonymity
have been accelerated by the extraordinary pressure in parts of
Wales for out-of-town shopping centres, with all the inevitable
ancillary developments such as car-parks, filling-stations, drive-in
burger-bars, hotels and warehouses. Indeed, the boast from
Tesco's UK management is that soon, if the planners do their jobs
properly, nobody in Britain should be more than a five-minute
drive from a superstore.

Nowhere is this trend more vividly expressed than in the western approach to Cardiff. Put simply, the city used to have a definite
beginning. Drivers emerged from the countryside of the Vale of
Glamorgan and were at once within the metropolitan confines of
Ely. The capital's identity was immediately, if not particularly
prepossessingly, apparent. But no more. The western approach is
now confused by a succession of roundabouts, feeder roads, super-
markets and other colossal and what could be prejudically termed
as glaringly inappropriate developments. Welcome to Cardiff is
Welcome to Tesco, a melancholy arrangement for those who love
the city, and almost as insulting as the grotesque and infantile
'Toys R Us' aircraft hangar, which is what currently greets the
visitor to Swansea's eastern centre.

The problem for the planners is that even when an out-of-town
superstore proposal is turned down, on grounds such as intrusion
into the countryside, or that it is not in keeping with the local plan,
the developers often appeal and then go to Public Inquiry. In about
fifty per cent of such cases, the original decision is thrown out, and
the store is built. As in the re-development of Swansea's 'maritime
quarter', and everywhere else it appears in the UK where docklands are redesigned, or in the scores of proposed out-of-town
hypermarket sites, the 'pagoda' or bell-tower style of construction
is much to the fore. This has replaced the previous favourite, the
'big shed' design, which for sheer architectural philistinism and
rampaging short-termism, was unmatchable.

As to stopping the superstores, environmentalists should broaden their campaign tactics. There is more mileage to be gained from illustrating that many of the jobs in such places will be badly-paid and part-time, and that trainees on initiatives such as Employment Training will be mercilessly exploited, than in complaining about loss of habitats for redstarts or great-crested newts. (Realistically, campaigns against such stores should always combine such arguments.)

Nevertheless, the edges of our towns, and most of our motorway junctions, are becoming American-style blighted nowherevilles, drenched in neon enticements to the mobile consumer. This in turn sucks trade out of the already hard-up town centres, threatening the livelihoods of the last small businesses that provide local commerce with its distinctiveness. A clear example of this is the Sainsbury superstore, built on the western fringe of Chester, which has had a damaging effect on the smaller Welsh shopping centres off the A55. There is, in fact, a commercial ecology that also needs our respect and energy to help it thrive.

But nothing affects urban Wales — like urban anywhere — more than the motorcar. In this country, there are 1.2 million privately owned vehicles, and over 22 million in the UK as a whole. (The government predicts an increase in this figure by fifty per cent by the year 2010). Indeed, motor sales are taken as one of the crucial indicators of the 'health' of the general economy. Such traffic growth has necessitated initiatives such as Cardiff City Council's installation of a pollution monitoring device in St. Mary Street, one of its busiest thoroughfares. Other traffic pollution testing has occurred in Swansea.

It is therefore simple to discover if air pollutants such as carbon monoxide and nitrogen dioxide in the Welsh capital are exceeding World Health Organisation suggested levels. Air quality briefings are printed daily in the local press. As an exercise in environmental information, this is highly useful. And yet, the City Council has no coherent strategy for limiting the number of vehicles visiting the city centre, and has actually embarked on a new road-building programme, despite evidence that construction of new roads, instead of dealing with traffic congestion, simply attracts more vehicles. Overall, this is the equivalent of a doctor visiting a patient equipped only with a stethoscope. The doctor might discover something is wrong, but is powerless to offer a remedy.

With the scourge of asthma increasing dramatically in Wales, what is required are air quality monitoring devices in all our bigger towns. But until we adopt a coherent transport policy that makes it cheap, convenient and safe for people to make buses and trains their first travelling choice, we will be granted only the dubious privilege of knowing whether the air we are compelled to breathe when we visit Cardiff is actually doing us harm.

One limited approach to this problem has been the introduction of pedestrianised areas into our towns. The most famous examples in Wales are Queen Street, Cardiff, and the Quadrant area of Swansea. But perhaps the most aesthetically pleasing are in Ebbw Vale and Wrexham, where the ability to stroll or sit unthreatened by anxious traffic is a rare and real delight. In these places, there is a definite lifting of the widespread neurosis that afflicts so much of urban Wales, created largely by the difficulties and perils of finding parking accommodation within commercial areas. Provision of street furniture, children's play areas, flowers and trees and even theatrical events in pedestrianised zones can enhance the idea of 'community' and perhaps even of *cymortha* in our towns that the demands of the motorcar have long submerged.

It must be said that few areas of urban Wales are important for any essential architectural merit. The fixation with 'heritage' means that we have already annexed many of the ruins associated with the coal and metal industries and turned them into historical exhibitions. In some, such as the Sygun copper mine at Beddgelert, or Big Pit, Blaenavon, we can vicariously experience the working conditions of the miners. We become tourists in our own history. The few precious, non-official city buildings we possess — such as those in the Alexandra Road area of Swansea, and Mount Stuart Square in Cardiff — currently suffer neglect and inappropriate use. Yet compared with some of the council estates built in the 1960s, such places continue to fare remarkably well.

In fact, the comfortably weathered terraces of Splott and Adamsdown in the capital, possess a symmetry and apparent sturdiness that is a complete contrast to the permanently raw concrete corrals constructed much more recently. Even the litany of their names has contributed to the unique flavour of the 'Cardiff experience'; Zinc Street, Silver Street, Iron Street, Lead Street,

Topaz Street, Ruby Street, Emerald Street, Sapphire Street, Comet Street, Eclipse Street, Constellation Street, Star Street, Sun Street, Moon Street. In their way, such modest thoroughfares have been as integral a part of urban Wales as the lost grandeur of the mansions of Cathedral Road and the always slightly elevated colliery managers' residences in the valleys. Such names, admittedly imposed without consultation, put into perspective the anaesthetising Hazelmeads, Meadowcrofts and Lapwing Closes that now proliferate in urban Wales. A street name, our planners should remember, can relate a good deal about its local environment.

Yet to return to the problem, the Penrhys estate in the Rhondda, for example, was designed in the sixties on the principles of a Mediterranean mountain village. Even accounting for the psychedelic euphoria of the time, this was a bizarre flight of the architectural imagination. Today, it's a bad trip. Penrhys is a maze of primitively-lit and paved walkways that end in dismal enclosures for parked cars and refuse bins. One thousand feet above sea-level, three thousand people (one third of them children) inhabit one of the windiest settlements in Wales. Testament to the weather is the 1993 Public Inquiry into a proposed wind-park on nearby Mynydd Tyntyle.

Eight miles away, the Glyntaff Farm Estate near Pontypridd is in even worse shape. Designed by the company responsible for Penrhys, its sewers are crumbling, its pedestrian areas dark and intimidating alleyways, its population grimly resentful and disaffected. In a long series of community meetings here with residents in the eighties, I first learned how badly let down many Welsh people are by the planners and designers of our urban environment. In Glyntaff Farm, the roads were too narrow to admit refuse lorries. People therefore dumped their rubbish in communal concrete bunkers for a weekly collection. Inevitably a collection of dogs, high winds and local children ensured that much of the waste was blown over the estate. Another interesting design feature was the omission of drying areas in the flats for wet clothes. Thus families were reduced to hanging washing out of windows.

Yet perhaps worse than this was the allocation of garden space to householders. In Glyntaff Farm, only a pavement's width was available to each new dwelling. The houses themselves, as in

Penrhys, were clustered as densely as possible together, with almost no thought given to sound proofing or individual privacy. The result is that children are either kept indoors, or must play out of sight of the parents, amidst the surreally-graffitied garage forecourts, vandalised bus-shelters and rubbish skips. For many residents, the temptation, in fact the solution to life in such places, is a recourse to the pacifying delights of video culture and satellite TV. How green was my valium, indeed.

The people of Penrhys, Glyntaff, Gurnos, the demolished abominations of Rose Row in Cwmbach and The Saltings at Briton Ferry, and countless other estates in urban South Wales and industrialised Clwyd, might well feel themselves the victims of cavalier environmental experimentation — despite the obvious need of local authorities to replace insanitary and cramped Welsh housing that might have dated from the previous century. The miners' tin baths and backyard privies were not myths. This is one reason why high profile yet mainstream environmental organisations hold such little sway in these areas. Considering that the Welsh Office estimates that the supply of suitable land, calculated for the period 1991 to 1997, is sufficient for the construction of over 60,000 new houses in Wales[1], this lack of popular pressure group influence is highly worrying.

Friends of the Earth, for example, has not a single local group on Deeside or in the entire extent of the South Wales valleys, apart from the lower Swansea Valley. Taking into account the efforts of FoE to demonstrate that its campaigns on contaminated land, 'greening' local authorities, air pollution's effects on human health, recycling and urban sprawl are entirely relevant to the urban majority, this is a damning admission. Even more surprising is that in many Welsh towns, such as superstore-blitzed Bridgend, the organisation that should have been an influence for environmental caution, the Civic Trust, has been conspicuous only by its absence.

Apart from under-informed and backyard-motivated residents' groups, there has too often been nothing to interfere with what has appeared as an unholy alliance between developers and planners to distort community identity, encourage uniformity and commercial gigantism, promote ugliness and reward falsity. And if such a conspiracy theory is nonsense, the only other explanation for our present predicament (at least for this writer) is consistent and finally unbearable pressure from the rapacious (the developers) on the ignorant and the gullible (the planners).

To be fair, there exist certain environmental initiatives on the more notorious housing estates in Wales. (And on some of those unsung but equally afflicted.) Yet it cannot be pretended that local people have created them. Rather, practical project-based organisations such as Groundwork and Community Service Volunteers have prepared strategies for clean-ups which involve local citizens' groups. This is commendable but often effective only on the 'scouts and guides' level. When they become more ambitious the inevitable question occurs of whether polluting industry or bad planners are having their mistakes rectified on the cheap.

Thus overall, there is much to be regretted about our present urban environment. But such feeling should not exclude optimism and a certain relief. Merthyr Tydfil in the 1830s epitomised everything that today we would consider as typical of the seeming anarchic squalor of a Rio de Janeiro *favela*. Life expectancy was low, there was staggering incidence of childhood illness. Almost a century later, the basic problems remained. In 1911 in Aberdare, for instance, child mortality was measured at 213 deaths per 1,000 births, compared with an England and Wales average of 122. Twenty years earlier, the Rhondda Medical Officer of Health had written that a local river contained "a large proportion of human excrement,...manure, congealed blood, offal and entrails... the rotten carcasses of animals... ashes, street refuse". He added that "in dry weather... the stench becomes unbearable".

Moreover, in the notorious Merthyr ghetto known as 'China', law and order was effectively thwarted by the influence of tavern culture. For generations in the coalfields, appalling standards persisted as the norm, created largely by unsafe working conditions and lack of nourishing food, clean water and sewage systems. Indeed, for a significant proportion of this century, the Welsh urban environment and its demands upon families were responsible for rendering the lives of the majority as miserable and deprived. Historically, woman and children perhaps suffered more than men. A coroner complained in 1920 that he held more inquests on miners' children who had been scalded to death in fireside baths than he did on colliers killed at work.[2] It was also estimated that the main cause of premature births in South Wales arose from pregnant women carrying heavy pails of hot water for their menfolk to wash after returning from the pit.[3]

Yet despite the ex-miners racked by pneumoconiosis, the estimated twelve thousand contaminated land sites, the millions of tons of slate and coal waste that lie on our hillsides, the unhealable wound of Aberfan — that blind revenge of the environment for our stupidity and abuse — urban Wales, at least in health and opportunity of its people, is a better place to live than ever before. There are salmon in the Taff again, the Dee is one of the most ecologically rich of UK estuaries, and otter spraints are discovered consistently lower down the Usk. Yet the myth of a pristine countryside has long gone, helped on its way by discoveries such as those of PCBs, mercury and other industrial pollution in the eggs of birds found in our most remote mountain ranges and headwaters.[4]

Wales will never be Holland. Or Essex. Or Baden Wurttenburg. However, it might aspire to become one of the so-called 'motor regions' of the EU. Would we relish the role? It remains unimaginable that we will impose a hygienic green regime on our surroundings and people. The roughness, the pollution, a well-developed sense of life's dangers, and a profound degree of environmental ignorance will persist in Wales.

The fact is that outside those formidable Welsh-speaking bastions of Bethesda, Blaenau Ffestiniog and Caernarfon, our urban environment is one that is sloughing its distinctive cultures — in both languages. Perhaps it is this above all which suggests a void at the heart of the new, 'prestigious' urban Wales of Cardiff Bay, superstores and heritage (whose heritage?) theme-parks. Meanwhile distinct working-class communities such as Ely in Cardiff appear beset by levels of crime and social tension that are amongst the most malevolent sources of environmental harm. If all that groups like Groundwork, Friends of the Earth and the Civic Trust can lobby for in these places are traffic calming schemes and recycling banks, they will deservedly continue to be ignored.

Notes

1. Environmental Digest for Wales, No. 7, Welsh Office.
2. *Glamorgan Historian*.
3. *Ibid*.
4. 1990 Study by the University of Wales College of Cardiff and the RSPB.

Alwyn Jones

'Beyond Environmentalism' — the Imperatives of 'Green' Philosophy

My concern for the environment can be traced back to the early sixties when I was working as an accountant in the Fiji Islands. Although I could have taken other travel opportunities open to me, in Europe and South America for instance, I chose Fiji because it appeared to offer an insight into a way of life *relatively* unspoiled by the impact of modern industrial society. My decision to go was influenced by the many authors, artists and poets who had travelled in the Pacific Islands and depicted in their various works how the islanders had managed to remain in harmony with the natural world despite the pressures of modernity. Perhaps nowhere is this harmony better represented than in the art of Paul Gaugin who deserted his native France to live, and die, in French Polynesia. Every time I see one of Gaugin's paintings of Polynesia it reminds me of what I believe to be his critical message: that the spirituality arising from the communion with nature which the Pacific Islanders enjoy is a world which we in the West have lost. It will be central to the argument in this chapter that the resolution of environmental problems cannot be achieved without the reassertion of the spiritual dimension of human life.

In Fiji I was fortunate to be able to spend some of my spare time in the highland villages on the main island of Viti Levu. What struck me on these visits was the extent to which the Fijians were

living in a way which minimised their dependence on industrialised production. Their houses were constructed almost entirely
from renewable materials directly obtained from the forest; fresh
clean water ran in the streams; the climate favoured the growth of
crops; transport was by foot, horse or river; and their social arrangements, based on family and community values, gave them a
sense of permanence and security. In modern environmental par-
lance it *was* a sustainable society. I say 'was' because when living
in Fiji I was fully aware of the extent to which western materialistic
values were making inroads into Fijian culture, and it can only be
assumed that this has gathered momentum since that time, as it
has in virtually every other part of the world.

I neither want to give the impression that Fijian life is without
difficulties and limitations, nor suggest that it is an ideal for which
it would be possible to aim in our own society. That would be most
unrealistic because circumstances are very different. But it does
give us a basis for reflection, as it did for me in the early 1960s. It
showed that it is possible for a human society to minimise its
physical impact on the environment, without necessarily undermining the *qualitative* dimension of human existence. This is in
almost total contrast to industrial society in which maximum
environmental impact is assumed to enhance the quality of life,
with the use of quantitative measuring devices such as 'gross
national product' giving positive support to this contention. On
such evidence Fiji would be regarded as poor or 'undeveloped'
because it has not 'enjoyed' the material progress of the 'advanced'
countries. But non-material or spiritual factors such as the quality
of children's play space, and the preservation of community values, on which Fiji would be much more highly rated than industrial society, are not included in these measurements of well-being.
This exposes the grave limitations of our techniques of measure-
ment, and reflects the precedence given to material over other
human values in industrial culture.

The Decline of Reason

This emphasis on materialistic values underlies the widely accepted belief in industrial societies that human betterment can be

achieved through economic growth and expansion, and gives legitimacy to the control and manipulation of nature in pursuit of these aims. I want to argue that this stress on materiality at the expense of other human goals, such as the spiritual and the aesthetic, has become a destabilising influence in the culture. In particular it has meant the development of a fragmented world view by the narrowing down of reason so that instrumental concerns are given priority over all other considerations.

We can differentiate between a substantive or all-encompassing reason which includes an evaluation of goals and purposes, and a *technical* reason which focuses specifically on the *means* by which a particular objective is to be achieved. As an example, let us consider the case of a civil engineer, specialised in motorway construction, who is contracted to construct a new motorway over a particular tract of country. The engineer will apply his/her skills in the building of the motorway in accordance with the most advanced technical knowledge currently available, but will not be required to evaluate the objective itself. For instance, the building of the motorway may entail the loss of prime agricultural land; it will encourage further vehicles onto the road thus adding to the problem of CO_2 emissions and other forms of pollution; and may require the demolition of residential dwellings in its path. Such considerations will not come within the engineer's brief which will be limited to ensuring that the most efficient means are used in the construction of the project. This is not to say that attention will not be paid to such factors at the planning stage, but it is unlikely that they would be given priority in the light of the *economic* objectives the motorway would be expected to fulfil. Such reasoning is not just confined to specific areas of social life, but tends to be pervasive in the culture as a whole. For instance, a hospital might discharge its patients as quickly as possible after treatment in order to improve its cost effectiveness, even though such action could be in conflict with the patient's best interest. The outcome of this is that instrumental considerations such as efficiency and utility become goals in themselves — means usurp ends — whilst human goals, values and purposes are not subjected to reason's critical gaze.

The Rise of Science

Technical reason is inextricably linked with science, the development of which owes much to the seventeenth century philosophers Descartes and Bacon. For Descartes there was a duality between an externalised material world and Mind or consciousness. By separating Mind from Matter in this way, nature is seen as a thing apart, inert and lifeless, but subject to laws which, once discovered, can put it under the control of humankind. Indeed, as Bacon argued, scientific knowledge was not to be the mere object of contemplation, but should be used as the instrument by which humankind could gradually attain mastery over nature in the pursuance of its own interests. Bacon saw the human/nature relationship as confrontational: nature was treated as an antagonist who would not willingly give up her secrets, and had to be 'bullied' into submission within controlled experimental conditions determined by the human observer. Perceived in this way scientific knowledge becomes the crucial mechanism for the promotion of technical reason: it is regarded not as an end, but as a means, expressed and applied in technology, by which humans assume power over the material world.

The principle of *analysis* lies at the centre of the scientific method. By making observations of *selected* parts or aspects of reality the scientist seeks to uncover causal connections between them within the framework of universally applicable laws and theories. Priority is thus given to the parts over the whole. The model of reality which emerges from this, as first suggested by Descartes, is of a vast machine-like world which can be understood by an analysis of its parts and the laws which govern their making. The fragmentary nature of such knowledge reinforces the pragmatism of modern industrial culture: for instance we apply chemicals on the land to increase crop yield; we administer drugs to treat disease; and we construct nuclear power stations to generate electricity. We take this action because it is *expedient* to do so in the light of the *specialised* scientific knowledge which we have at our disposal, but this will be at the expense of being unable to predict with any degree of accuracy what will be the overall implications of our actions. And as our 'mastery' over nature increases, and the general level of our activities intensify, the life support systems upon which we depend for our survival are put under ever greater threat. We cannot know when the critical point will be reached because we are basing our actions on a theory of knowledge which gives us only a partial view of reality.

The Consumerist Ethic

In my earlier reference to Fiji I made the point that the Fijian way of life as I experienced it in the early 1960s impacted only minimally on the physical environment. In their closeness to nature the Fijians appeared to be intuitively aware of the extent to which they depended on it for the continuance of life. But in industrial society, and increasingly everywhere else, most people live in urban areas and are out of harmony with the natural world. If they think about it at all, nature is a 'resource' to be exploited, something 'out there' of which they do not see themselves a part. Yet they are no less dependent on the preservation of nature than people living in the highland villages of Fiji. The difference lies in the extent to which the urban and the rural have become separate domains in modern society, thus desensitising the urban dweller from an awareness of the patterns and rhythms of nature. Even in the rural areas the traditional community structures have broken down with the advent of modern chemicalised industrial farming techniques. And for those few who still remain working on the land, such techniques draw people away from direct contact with the earth, and undermine the reciprocal interaction between the human being and nature which lay at the centre of traditional farming practices. The attenuation of ties with the land, and the undermining of community values, have meant that consumerism has progressively become a key feature of advanced industrial societies. The implications of this are profound and have to be given central place in any discussion of environmental imperatives.

A key feature of an industrial system based on ever-expanding levels of production is the way in which people identify the satisfaction of need with the *consumption* of commodities. As the neo-Marxist thinker Herbert Marcuse[1] has argued, the 'technological' rationality of modern society has made possible the continual creation of new (false) needs, which become perceived *as* needs in human consciousness. The belief is widespread that the 'good' life is obtained by the maximisation of expenditure on the goods and services produced by society's institutions. Not only does the standard of living become almost entirely defined in material terms, but consumption becomes an end in itself, with the result that consumers are tied to their possessions, and to a consumerist ideology upon which the expansion of industrial society depends. That this is the conventional wisdom of our day has been well borne out during the current recession in which the Government is continually looking for evidence that High Street sales are picking up, the assumption being that this is the prime indicator of our overall well-being. No attempt is made to question consumption patterns, or to ask what goods are being bought in the shops and whether people really need them. Indeed such questions would be tantamount to heresy in a consumer-driven society.

The pervasiveness of consumerism in modern society has been well illustrated in the writings of the social critic Ivan Illich. I have shown earlier how the paramountcy of technical reason effectively silences debate over the goals or purposes of life, with the result that efficiency and utility virtually become goals in themselves in the furtherance of output maximisation. For Illich this process is given its *institutional* expression in the emergence of the modern bureaucratic organisation. Indeed the bureaucracy, backed by scientific knowledge, and aided by professional expertise, becomes the means by which the questions addressed by technical reason are resolved.

It was perhaps the sociologist Max Weber who first recognised the extent to which technical reason, or what he called formal rationality, had its outward manifestation in the bureaucratic organisation. For him the development of bureaucracy in modern life meant the erosion of substantive human values such as spontaneity, autonomy, freedom and democracy. The extreme negativity to which this leads us is expressed poignantly in the following passage: "Specialists without spirit, sensualists without heart; this nullity imagines that it has attained a level of civilisation never before achieved".[2]

Illich has extended Weber's somewhat generalised critique of rationality and bureaucracy by placing the accompanying phenomenon of professionalisation at the centre of his analysis of industrialism. For him the rapid growth of a technocratic elite, equipped with a professional and technological expertise from which the lay person is excluded, has meant that bureaucratic institutions have increasingly become controlled by professionals who establish the criteria for the determination and meeting of needs. This is what Illich means by the 'institutionalisation of values', a process by which the institutional imposition of values (needs) by professional edict erodes the freedom of individuals to create their own needs in a meaningful community setting. Human beings are turned into consumers who come to perceive that "whatever good there is, is the product of some specialised institution".[3] Illich believes that all the more important spheres of life have been affected by this process, for instance in education, medicine, transport and religion as well as the production of industrial products.

For Illich, school plays a pivotal role in the inculcation of the consumerist ethos in modern industrial society. We have come to believe that learning is possible only in the school or other educational institution, and that its value increases with the amount of input measured by certificates at different levels of education. Increasingly, employers expect higher qualifications than formerly, with the result that work that could be done with GCSE or its equivalent in the past now requires 'A' level or even a degree. This means a steadily upwards spiral of demand for education which becomes a commodity to be purchased from an institution rather than an independent learning process. To be regarded as 'well-educated' a person will have had to 'consume' a large number of educational credits over many years of institutionalised learning. Once people perceive that the only way to learn is through a teacher-directed educational process, the greater is the likelihood that they will succumb to the dominance of a highly professionalised technostructure oriented to meet *all* essential needs. Illich is in no doubt that this has occurred in the modern world. For instance: "medical treatment is mistaken for health care, social work for the improvement of community life, [and] police protection for safety".[4]

Illich's analysis of the structure of industrial society gives us an important insight into the way in which institutions have been externalised, and made inaccessible, spiritually, morally and cognitively, to the people as a whole. The fragmentation of culture to which this gives rise means that individuals can no longer relate together and independently determine their needs in a *community* setting from which life derives its meaning and purpose. Moreover the association of value creation with the products of institutions means that people are left with little alternative other than to maximise their consumption, whether this be of goods or services. The scenario which emerges is one in which the qualitative dimension of human life is redefined in quantitative terms. For example, health is defined by the number of doctors or by medical technology available; movement by the number of cars or other vehicles on the road; learning by the level and quantity of educational credits obtained; and entertainment by the possession of TV sets or other appropriate electronic technologies. The spiritual impoverishment which this reflects is well summarised by Illich: "In such an intensely industrialised society, people are conditioned to *get* things rather than to *do* them; they are trained to value what can be purchased rather than what they themselves can create. They want to be taught, moved, treated or guided rather than to learn, to heal, and to find their own way. Impersonal institutions are assigned personal functions".[5]

The relentlessness with which consumption is pursued leads not only to the draining of life's spiritual content and meaning, but also to social and ecological destabilisation. It is currently argued by some in the green movement that equilibrium can be restored insofar as we put on to the market only those products which are passed as 'environmentally friendly'. But leaving aside the question whether a consensus can be reached on the establishment of the appropriate criteria for this notion, paradoxically called 'green consumerism', it will do nothing to reduce the *overall* demands placed on the planet's life support systems. Indeed the enthusiasm for 'greening' which is springing up almost everywhere in the industrial world is a thinly veiled disguise for a 'business as usual' approach. Whilst it is not the intention to decry the efforts of those in government, industry and elsewhere who are now beginning to take account of environmental factors in the decision-making process, it is my view that they do not go far enough. Such token gestures are classic examples of the way in which technical reason is applied to current environmental problems. For instance lead is extracted from petrol, but cars are kept on the road; 'environmentally friendly' products are introduced onto the market, but businesses are encouraged to grow; and safety regulations are tightened after an industrial disaster such as Chernobyl, without steps being taken to abandon nuclear power. What these examples show is the extent to which policy makers and others are prepared to take action on an *ad hoc* basis without questioning the overall physical, social, political and economic context within which such problems arise. As long as the ultimate priority remains the furtherance of material growth there can be no place for consideration of questions wider than the specific technical issues involved.

The Environmentalist Response

So far I have hesitated to mention Wales specifically because in any discussion of green philosophy it is first necessary to grasp some of the essential features of the environmental debate. Once parameters for the analysis have been established it becomes easier to set the substantive issues being raised in this book within their overall context. We are right to give consideration to matters which are of particular concern for Wales, but we must not lose sight of the fact that there are no geographical or other boundaries to environmental problems. Indeed most people are now well aware that phenomena such as acid rain, planetary warming and ozone depletion have global implications and need a global response. But what is perhaps less realised is the extent to which apparently 'local' issues cannot be properly assessed without widening the basis of our understanding. For instance it is not necessary to travel far in South Wales to appreciate that there is a serious problem of litter in both town and country areas. The Keep Wales Tidy Campaign does a very effective job in keeping down the level of litter, and raising awareness among the community as a whole with its excellent publicity campaigns. But the limitation of its brief as a *single issue* pressure group does not allow it to set the litter problem within a broader frame of reference. Over the past few years the growth of groups like the Keep Wales Tidy Campaign has been a characteristic of the green movement, whether in Wales or elsewhere, thereby enabling action to be taken on a wide range of environmental issues. But by treating each environmental threat as a separate issue, to which we make a specific response, we avoid having to take into consideration the possibility of making radical changes to the way in which we live our lives.

The single-issue or environmentalist approach to the ecological problems we face today is based on the assumption that enlightened management of the Earth and its resources will make possible the continuance of the industrial way of life. This recalls the mechanistic conception of the Earth discussed in my earlier reference to Descartes, in which the parts are given priority over the whole, everything being understood in terms of universally applicable laws discovered by science. It is presumed that if we keep the 'machine' in good order by appropriate environmental maintenance, we stand a good chance not only of protecting the environment for those of us alive today, but also for countless generations to come. But can this contention be substantiated?

It is ironic that the twentieth century challenges to this piecemeal understanding of the Earth should come from within science itself at a time when advances in science and technology had made possible an unparalleled period of industrial expansion. I am referring in particular to quantum theory in physics, and more recently James Lovelock's Gaia hypothesis.

The Relevance of Quantum Theory

I have already discussed the relationship between quantum theory and 'green' thought in two articles in *The Ecologist* in 1987 and 1988, and it would not be appropriate to develop it further in detail here.[6] However, the picture of the *sub-atomic* world which emerges from quantum theory is of a never-ending series of energy exchanges between atomic particles. Unlike the classical mechanistic view of reality in which *isolated* particles relate together *externally* to make the whole, quantum reality is characterised by the total *interconnectedness* of particles which *inter-relate reciprocally* so that the parts become *indistinguishable* from the whole. Moreover the discovery that changes in sub-atomic reality take place spontaneously and unpredictably, in discontinuous quantum 'leaps' or 'jumps', is in contrast to the widely held view of mechanistic science that no change can take place other than causally with effects following causes in ever flowing linear time. Another assertion of quantum theory which is very important for our purposes, is that particles have the capacity to spread out in space in wave-like fashion. Whilst this raises profound questions about the ultimate nature of reality, the wave capacity that particles possess means that everything is connected to everything else. In such circumstances a change in any one part of the whole has a potential effect on every other part even though the parts are distanced from each other both in time and space. But because we are dealing with the whole, which for the quantum theorist is the *only* reality, we are not in a position to predict the effect on it of any changes in the inter-relationships among the parts.

Quantum theory is of course concerned with microscopic reality and it can be argued that it has no relevance to the material world as we experience it at the macroscopic level. Indeed we cannot do without some notion of causality in order to get on with our everyday lives. For instance we take care when we are driving because we can predict with some degree of accuracy what would happen if we crashed into another car; we can play games like tennis or snooker because we know what has to be done to set the balls in motion; and we refrain from putting a hand into the heat of a fire. All these examples relate to our understanding of *simple* cause and effect relationships with which we are very familiar. It is in areas such as this that the mechanistic approach serves us well.

But once we take a broader view the picture changes dramatically. From a quantum perspective even the striking of a tennis or snooker ball would have implications for the whole of reality, but in the unlikely event of our wishing to know what these would be there would be no basis available to us on which predictions could be made. This is, of course, a trivial example and of no importance in our daily lives. But we would be no better placed to make predictions when faced with much bigger issues such as evaluating the overall environmental impact of applying chemical fertilisers in agriculture, or using nuclear power as a source of energy. Mechanistic science can tell us a great deal about the relationship between crop yield and a particular fertiliser, but is virtually silent on the long or medium term effects of fertiliser use. Such questions are too generalised to be raised under the controlled circumstances of laboratory experimentation. Similarly with nuclear power: whereas much is known about the properties of specific radio-active isotopes from experiments carried out under controlled conditions, we can be no more than speculative as to what is a safe level of radiation, or what risks to which we and future generations are subjected as a result of having nuclear activities going on in our midst. Examples such as these both expose the inherent weakness of a scientific approach which emphasises the part at the expense of the whole, and indicate the considerable extent to which insights gained from quantum theory at the microscopic level of reality are equally applicable in the macroscopic world of everyday experience.

The Gaia Hypothesis

Quantum theory's assertion of oneness at the microscopic level of reality is reflected by a similar assertion at the macroscopic level by the independent chemist, James Lovelock,[7] whose Gaia hypothesis has become extremely important in the green movement in recent years. The basic claim of the hypothesis is that the Earth is a single *living* organism in which all its parts inter-relate co-operatively to create and sustain the whole. Lovelock's meta-phorical use of Gaia, the ancient Greek goddess of the Earth, aptly expresses this notion of the Earth as a living entity. *Mother* Earth is not merely the source of Life, but also the process by which Life is nurtured and sustained. Such sustainability is made possible through regulatory mechanisms built into the organism which enable it to resist adverse environmental changes, in much the same way as perspiration stabilises the temperature of the body when it becomes overheated.

It is a fundamental tenet of the hypothesis that *Life* did not adapt to already pre-existing conditions, but *itself* created the conditions which made it possible for it to be sustained. It is argued that the various life forms which inhabit the *biosphere* — the wafer-thin part of the Earth's crust which surrounds the surface of the planet —

inter-relate together to ensure the continuance of life. For instance the delicate balance of the major gases in the atmosphere — at seventy-nine per cent nitrogen, twenty-one per cent oxygen and 0.03 per cent carbon dioxide — must be maintained if life is not to be threatened. Even a small increase in the proportion of oxygen in the atmosphere would lead to continuous combustion; likewise the concern over global warming arises from minimal increases which have been shown to be taking place in carbon dioxide and other atmospheric gases. According to Lovelock, and his associate and co-author of the hypothesis, Lynn Margulis, an American professor of microbiology, practices such as plant photosynthesis, and carbon burial on sea and on land, are examples of how different organisms act as regulatory mechanisms which contribute to the maintenance of atmospheric equilibrium as a crucial aspect of the Earth's life support systems. Margulis, in particular, has stressed the extent to which micro-organisms such as bacteria, which we so readily associate with disease, have a major regulatory role to play in making Gaia a suitable place for the existence of life.

It might seem that because of the existence of regulatory mechanisms, Gaia can deal with any perturbations which threaten the continuity of existing patterns of life on Earth. But this is not necessarily so. As Lovelock has argued, the stress on Gaia may be so great that *current* regulatory processes can no longer cope with the situation. Whereas this may threaten the existing range of species, including ourselves, it does not mean the extinction of Gaia. Both Lovelock and Margulis argue that a new Gaian equilibrium would eventually be established without those life forms, particularly *Homo sapiens*, which had previously threatened Gaia's survival. This raises a major environmental question: are our current activities leading to irreversible changes in the existing Gaian arrangements of life on Earth?

Lovelock does not think that we have yet reached the point of irreversibility, despite mounting evidence of planetary-wide problems such as global warming and the weakening of the ozone barrier. But the pressure we are putting on the Gaian life support systems is *cumulative*, and we may well reach a point at which it is no longer possible for the current regulatory mechanisms to contain the existing equilibrium. Indeed, as Lovelock says, if we persist with our 'planetary experiments', of which deforestation is perhaps the most hazardous, we may well have to face up to the ultimate Gaian response.

Both Quantum theory and the Gaia hypothesis give priority to the whole over the part. They show up the weaknesses of the conventional scientific approach by emphasising the unpredictability of reality at their respective levels of analysis. Moreover they both stress the inseparability of observer and observed. For instance I mentioned earlier that sub-atomic particles can behave either as waves or particles; but how they behave depends on the way in which they are perceived by the observer. If perceived as waves, they behave as waves; if as particles, they behave as particles. In quantum theory the observer is no longer neutral and detached, but inextricably *participating* in the experimental process itself. And the same goes for Gaia. *Homo sapiens* does not stand outside the world as a disinterested observer trying, in Baconian fashion, to wrestle nature's secrets from her. Instead we are part of the whole and subject to the same Gaian processes as all other forms of life. Our participative role, and the fact that we cannot predict what the ultimate outcome of our actions will be, give us no grounds on which we can presume to take control over the natural world. A science-backed technical reason must give way to a new framework for understanding in which the aim is to co-operate with nature rather than control it. In such circumstances no distinction can be made between science and ethics, and concern for the environment will become indistinguishable from the scientific process itself.

But we are far removed from a world in which a new standpoint such as this can be adopted. Indeed the consumerist ethos which lies at the heart of industrialism, and which we discussed in earlier references to Marcus and Illich, is now planetary-wide, making our survival in the existing Gaian order of things ever more problematic. The 'greening' of consumption may slow down the rate at which we approach the apocalypse but it will not stop it. Catalytic converters, CFC-free refrigerators, and environmental management systems are all very well, but they do not get to the core of the problem: the nature of industrialism itself. Until we turn away from the materialist orientations on which industrial expansion depends, we are not going to usher in an age in which our lifestyles and social arrangements are consistent with Gaian principles. Yet that must be the major task which faces us in the world today.

Social Limits to Growth

I began with a reference to my sojourn in the Fiji Islands in the early 1960s. I did this because in Fiji, and in some other parts of the Pacific, I saw before me a way of life which was spiritually vibrant despite the minimal demands placed upon nature. It made me think that it was possible to live a satisfactory and fulfilling life without the excessive material gadgetry of modern life. But I did not think then, as I do now, of the deeper implications of this dependence on material growth. Not only are there *physical* limits to our perturbation of the Gaian world, but *social* constraints, which go largely unrecognised, emerge as well. Illich's institutionalisation of values in which human freedom is systematically eroded by the ever-increasing dependence on the products of institutions for the meeting of need, is a case in point.

Another perspective on the social implications of growth has been advanced by the economist Fred Hirsch in his important book *Social Limits to Growth*.[8] For Hirsch, a paradox lies at the heart of the commitment to unrestrained industrial expansion: once a certain point has been reached the further production of a particular service or commodity leads to a deterioration in the quality of its use by the consumer. For instance, the relative value to an individual of owning a motorcar, or having access to higher education, is dependent on how many other people are equally favoured. As more and more people come to own motorcars, the conditions of road use for each individual deteriorates; similarly with increasing access to educational opportunities individuals will have to obtain higher qualifications to retain their present position relative to everybody else. The position a person holds in what Hirsch describes as the 'positional economy' is thus a precarious one in a society committed to continual growth. The effect of this will be the reinforcement of existing class and other divisions in society as people compete relentlessly for scarce *positional* resources.

Hirsch's assertion that there are social limits to growth adds a new *qualitative* dimension to the environmental debate. Whereas physical aspects of the debate are open to *ad hoc* technological 'fix' solutions, however inadequate they may be, no such solutions are possible once we move into the social domain. Indeed by suggesting that beyond a certain point our activities are counterproductive, both Hirsch and Illich are raising profound philosophical questions about the whole basis of life in industrial society. They are forcing out into the open the contradictory nature of the industrial process, and challenging the values upon which the whole edifice rests. Once this analysis is seen in the context of the insights gained from quantum theory and the Gaia hypothesis, which expose the shortcomings of mechanistic science, the full extent of the ecological dilemma which we face today comes vividly into focus.

The Imperative of 'Green' Philosophy

The imperative of 'green' philosophy is that nothing short of a new paradigm, a complete change of direction, will suffice if this dilemma is to be resolved. As both Quantum theory and Gaia show us, reality is based on co-operation and inter-relatedness, yet the modern world has fragmented family and community which were the basis of mutualism and reciprocity in human relationships. The undermining of the spiritual and ethical dimensions of human life which this implies is reinforced by the institutional determination of needs and values, and people are left with virtually no alternative but to search for meaning in the material realm of human existence. Such a society, which ignores the diversity and richness of human experience, is, as Illich puts it, "dynamically unstable. It is organised for indefinite expansion and the concurrent unlimited creation of new needs, which in an industrial environment soon become basic necessities".[9]

The extreme specialisation of the rational mind in industrial societies has suppressed our powers of intuition which alone enable us to grasp the 'oneness' of all things. The first step towards a new paradigm in the existing world order must therefore be the recovery of intuition, and the broadening of reason, so that from the interplay between them philosophical principles can be established for the emergence of a green future. A key feature of this, as we have seen from Quantum theory and Gaia, will be the recognition that interconnectedness and interdependence lie at the basis of reality. Once we perceive ourselves as part of the *one* reality any abuse of nature to which our activities give rise will at the same time be seen as an abuse of ourselves. By way of illustration, let me take just one example from my experience in Wales: Maendy Quarry near Pontypridd. The toxic wastes dumped many years ago in this quarry to the west of the University of Glamorgan, bear witness to this day of the deplorable suffering of the Earth at our hands. Every time I see that quarry, and I have seen it many times, I can almost feel the pain that the Earth must be enduring. By sharing in the Earth's trauma when it undergoes such deprivation we are preparing the ground for an expansion of consciousness in which human attitudes to the environment move from confrontation to participation.

Whilst the concept of participation with nature must be the key organising principle for a green future, it cannot be a reality until the appropriate social arrangements are in place. And here we come to our greatest difficulty. Many people have accused Greens of being too unrealistic and utopian in their thought, looking idealistically towards a future which we cannot hope to put into practice. I will be similarly categorised, particularly in my reference to Fiji. It will be said that Fijians want 'progress' as much as everyone else and to deny this to them is the height of Western arrogance. Be that as it may, I have tried to argue that the universal extension of Western materialism as we know it must come up against insurmountable limits. Even if we do accept that there will always be a 'scientific' answer to environmental problems arising from industrial expansion, once the question of *social* limits is raised there can be no such response. The green critique must therefore go beyond environmentalist rhetoric, that thinly disguised apologia for the existing order of things, and seek nothing less than the reconstitution of society itself.

A Convivial Society?

The fragmentation of the modern world into discrete and relatively autonomous institutional complexes is far removed from the reality of Gaia. If a future society based on the Gaian principles of interdependence, mutuality and inter-relatedness is to be achieved, as I believe it must, a re-emergence of some form of community is essential. Once more I turn to Illich, and in particular to his notion of 'conviviality' which emphasises the interconnectedness between the individual and social and physical reality through "autonomous and creative intercourse among persons, and the intercourse of persons with their environment... I consider conviviality to be individual freedom realised in personal interdependence and, as such, an intrinsic ethical value".[10]

A convivial society is based on a principle of *participative* justice in which freedom for one is equated with a like freedom for all. Unlike industrial society, in which the focus is on the achievement of the individual in isolation from others, conviviality emphasises the togetherness of human beings realising their creative potentialities within a framework of inter-relatedness. It is a society of relatively small scale because it is only in such circumstances that people are in a position to perceive the social and territorial boundaries of their reality, so that they feel a sense of bonding and place in it. This is the spiritual element, present in small communities, but lacking in the modern world. This will be familiar to people in Wales where there is a long tradition of community living, though such communities, especially in the urban areas, were vulnerable because they were too dependent on the success of one particular industry. In contrast to this, conviviality assumes a high degree of self-reliance in which all those tasks which make up a *meaningful* way of life are carried out at the level of the community. The richness and *diversity* to which this gives rise brings the social system into line with Gaia in which diversity ensures stability and continuity.

Conviviality has profound political and economic implications. Participative justice entails the empowerment of people at the grass-roots level through participative rather than representative democracy. The re-establishment of meaning arising from the

169

restoration of community provides a favourable climate for direct political participation, but no blueprint can be laid down for the institutional processes within which this will take place. Institutions will simply *evolve* in accordance with the perceived needs of the community, but because they arise *from within* will remain subject to grass-roots control. In the economic sphere the resurgence of local markets, and the closing of the gap between buyer and seller, will reflect the greater self-reliance and autonomy at the community level emanating from convivial reconstruction.

A convivial society does *not* entail a return to an Arcadian past; but it *does* imply radically different approaches to our technologies so that they become fully accessible to every member of the community by adding to, and not detracting from, each person's potential for self-development and creativity insofar as this is consistent with community and environmental needs. For instance, conviviality recognises that information technology has a crucial role to play in the decentralisation of society, and the restoration of community life. The return to community does not mean turning our backs on technology, but redefining it so that it has an enhancing role rather than one of Frankensteinian mastery and control. Through the *enlightened* use of appropriate community technologies modern industrial society is potentially well-placed to advance towards a future in which the social integration enjoyed by a society such as Fiji can become a realistic alternative to the existing order of things. A visit to the Centre for Alternative Technology, Machynlleth, will indicate to sceptics and others that this is no utopian dream. The technologies are already available; what is lacking is the ethos which will allow us to move ahead.

Finally, the stipulation that interdependence is an 'intrinsic ethical value' has implications for the reformulation of human attitudes to social and physical reality. It means, in particular, that the assumed division between individuals and their physical and social environment collapses, with the result that co-operation, rather than competition, becomes the organising principle for social life. This brings conviviality close to Gaia which, as we have seen, claims that the Earth is a *single* 'living' organism in which the parts relate together symbiotically to create the whole. The scenario suggested by both conviviality and Gaia of an interconnected reality raises ethical issues of considerable importance. In particular, once we perceive our own well-being to be inextricably linked with that of the overall environment, no action can be taken without incurring moral responsibility.

Rising Ecological Consciousness

But we have so far failed to face up to our responsibilities. We have assumed that nature is an unlimited resource to be exploited at will, and that our own capacities are infinite. With mounting evidence that our profligate activities have brought us to the brink of planetary-wide ecological disaster, such claims are manifestly false. But, as I have indicated, a new philosophy is emerging, backed by recent developments in science, which gives some grounds for hope that there will be a breakthrough in 'green' thinking to take us beyond the narrow environmentalism with which we currently respond to ecological problems.

Let me conclude by speculatively suggesting the course this is likely to take. First, the insights gained from Quantum theory and the Gaia hypothesis give priority to the whole over the part and emphasise that there is only *one* interconnected reality. Our embeddedness in this reality unequivocally establishes the principle that all actions we take must be morally justified. Secondly, we have seen that there is no basis on which we can scientifically predict what will be the overall effect of our actions on the environment. The lessons of disasters such as Chernobyl and Bhopal, and insidious processes such as ozone depletion and global warming, will make us increasingly aware of the counterproductive and unpredictive tendencies of industrial growth and progress. Knowledge of such phenomena will reinforce the need to contain our activities at a scale at which we can retain ultimate control. Finally the ecological crisis will penetrate our consciousness as a crisis of values with an urgent need to transform existing social structures so that our lifestyles and institutions can mirror the processes we find in the natural world. Our ethical horizons must not however be limited to a particular locality, but must be expanded so that we embrace a planetary or even a cosmic consciousness. Without prejudice to the variety and diversity of cultural systems by which the human condition is punctuated world-wide, all cultures must identify with an overarching ecological consciousness without which the survival of the existing Gaian social order must forever remain in doubt.

Notes

1. Marcuse, H. *One Dimensional Man*, Abacus, 1972.
2. Weber, M. *The Protestant Ethic and the Spirit of Capitalism*, Unwin University Books, 1930, p.182.
3. Illich, I. *Deschooling Society*, Penguin, 1973, p.109.
4. *Ibid.*, p.9.
5. Illich, I. *Limits to Medicine*, Penguin, 1977, p.217.
6. Jones, A. 'From Fragmentation to Wholeness: A Green Approach to Science and Society (Part 1)', *The Ecologist*, Vol.17 (6), 1987, pp.236-240. Part 2, *The Ecologist*, Vol.18 (1), 1988, pp.30-34.
7. See Lovelock, J.E. *Gaia: A New Look at Life on Earth*, Oxford, 1979; and Lovelock, J. *The Ages of Gaia*, Oxford, 1988.
8. Hirsch, F. *Social Limits to Growth*, RKP, 1977.
9. Illich, I. *Tools for Conviviality*, Fontana, 1975, p.60.
10. *Ibid.*, p.24.

Alan Watson

Environmental Information and Wales: the Means for Change

W e have opened the door to environmental information" said John Major in 1991, heralding a new spirit of openness. "Every individual, every group, will in future have access to the information they need in order to act as an environmental watchdog. That information is the citizen's right, and the Active Citizen will use that right constructively" (Sunday Times Conference, 8 July 1991). It will be shown in this chapter that there is still a long way to go before the Prime Minister's claim becomes reality, but it is vitally important that we use the information already available. We must 'use it or lose it', for if we do not the pressure to reduce the facilities provided will mount.

The administrator of the United States Environmental Protection Agency has rightly said "the impact of the toxic release inventory [a publicly available database of emissions from industry] has far exceeded our expectations as a tool for improving environmental management... and *should be considered to be among the most important weapons in efforts to combat pollution*" (USEPA. 'Toxics in the Community, National and Local Perspectives' September 1991). In America the Chemical Industries Association has realised that public confidence can only be regained by a spirit of openness and they have launched a public awareness campaign with the slogan "don't trust us — track us!". It remains to be seen how long it will take for industry in Wales to follow suit.

In this chapter I propose to review the environmental information that is available, what is difficult to obtain, to show how to access it and what to do when you are blocked in your search. Finally, I have provided an overview of the statistics that examines some of the conservation measures and the threats to the environment of Wales.

Environmental Information

In an 'information age' there is a real danger of being flooded with piles of paper and becoming tied up in processing information rather than using it. Before embarking on collecting information it may be useful to ask:

Why do I want this information?
What information is available?
How do I get the information?
Where am I going to get the information from?

Why do I want this information?

The types of information required for a school project, a letter to a councillor about a local nuisance, a public inquiry into a potentially damaging new development or an inquisitive look at the emissions from a local factory will all appear to be quite different. However, there are likely to be important similarities: they may all be environmental information; the data obtained needs to be accurate and reliable if it is to be effective; and the methods of obtaining it may be the same.

Good information about the state of our environment, the emissions to it and the threats it faces is essential if we are to be able to become more fully involved in the protection of our environment. This was recognised in Agenda 21, the blueprint for global actions to effect the transition to sustainable development, that emerged from the Earth Summit in 1992.

What information is available? How do I get it? and Where am I going to get it from?

There is an increasing quantity of information available to us about the environment. Some of this is readily available at little or no cost but other information may be difficult and expensive to obtain.

Looking at the relative ease of access to information in turn:

A) Public Libraries.
Are likely to hold the main sets of statistics published by the Welsh Office and the Department of the Environment. Particularly useful are the Welsh Office publications *Environmental Digest for Wales* and *Welsh Transport Statistics* which are published annually by the Welsh Office and contain a mass of useful data about a wide range of environmental issues.

Less specific to Wales are the Department of the Environment publications. *Digest of Environmental Protection and Water Statistics* is dry but comprehensive, whilst *The UK Environment* is written in a user-friendly style but contains less raw data and tables. Also useful on the HMSO shelf are the annual reports for *This Common Inheritance* which give a review on the progress towards the targets set in the Government's White Paper on the Environment and includes a small section specifically about Wales. The Welsh Office publishes its own report, 'The Environment in Wales', which is almost the same as the Welsh section in the Government's annual reports but has the advantage of being bilingual.

Libraries are obviously also good sources of specific texts about technical and historic issues, of newspaper cuttings and of maps. Each of these can be essential for investigating subjects like contaminated land, which should have been available on a public register kept by local authorities by now. Unfortunately, the Government has backed down under pressure from the construction industry and has not yet implemented regulations to require registers on contaminated land to be drawn up. A detailed study of the information in a library, such as old maps and commercial directories, may sometimes be the only way of finding out what the previous use of a potentially contaminated piece of land has been (and hence establish the risk of contamination).

B) Other published information.
There is a wide range of more detailed information that is published by the Government and other bodies that will probably not be available in most libraries but could be ordered, seen at the copy-

right library in Aberystwyth or, if funds allow it, purchased.

Useful reports include those from the Welsh Affairs Committee and published by HMSO such as 'Toxic Waste Disposal in Wales'. Sections of this document are now slightly out of date but it is still a very good source of information. The Welsh Office also produces replies to these reports which can give a good indication of Government policy on the issues. On a similar line but not specifically directed at Wales are the publications of the House of Commons Environment Committee such as their reports 'Contaminated Land' and 'Toxic Waste'. In some cases, evidence has been given to the Committee by Welsh authorities which can be particularly useful. Evidence that has been presented to House of Commons Committees and not published in the final reports can be obtained from the libraries of the House of Commons or House of Lords.

The Royal Commission on Environmental Pollution has published eighteen reports covering a range of environmental issues from hazards of genetic engineering to freshwater pollution. These are often very good background papers and can contain information which is specific to Wales.

Less readily available are the more technical reports published by the now defunct Warren Springs Laboratory. These are expensive but provide detail about specific sites under study. An example is their 'Air Quality Audit — BP Chemicals, Baglan Bay' published in December 1992 and invaluable for anyone needing independent information about the emissions and operation of sites under study. The Welsh Office also occasionally commission similar studies and in 1993 they published the final report of the Panteg monitoring project, 'Polychlorinated Biphenyls, Dioxins and Furans in the Pontypool Environment' which concluded that the authors thought it was 'beyond reasonable doubt' that the Rechem plant was polluting the area around their incinerator with PCBs, Dioxins and Furans.

A small number of companies voluntarily provide information about their emissions (notably BP). If a member of the public is interested in obtaining such details it is always worth approaching the operator of a factory first.

Finally, organisations like Friends of the Earth Cymru produce environmental information covering a wide range of topics from wind energy to 'Plastic Objects Disposed to Sewers'. Their reports are bilingual and specifically directed at protecting the environment of Wales.

C) Public Registers

Unlike the ill-fated 'Registers of Land Subject to Potentially Contaminative Uses' (see above) other public registers of environmental information have been established. Unfortunately, few of them are widely used, largely because they are not well advertised, are often inconvenient to visit and are sometimes not user-friendly. Amongst the most useful for environmental information are:

i) National River Authority Registers

This register monitors results and flow rates for surface waters and, less comprehensively, groundwater (such as borehole results from around landfill sites) which have been sampled by the NRA. A written request for data may be sent but this can be expensive and may not provide exactly what is needed. Alternatively registers may be viewed without charge at a variety of NRA offices around Wales (hard copies of data may be charged for, however).

ii) Water Authority Registers

Everybody is entitled to a full report on the quality of their drinking water and this should be obtainable simply by writing to the water authority and asking them to forward a copy. No charge will be made for a report covering the applicant's own 'zone' but charges may be made for copies of reports for other areas. It is possible to visit the register at offices of the water companies in which case all records can be viewed without any charge.

iii) Registers of Waste Disposal licences

District and Borough Councils, generally the environmental health department, keep a register of all the licensed landfill and waste disposal sites (transfer stations, incinerators, civic amenity sites) in their areas. These show the conditions that must be met by the operators and details such as any statutory notices that may have been served on the operating company. No charge is made for access which is available during normal office hours.

iv) Integrated Pollution Control Applications
The 1990 Environmental Protection Act has introduced a new system of regulation for the more polluting industrial processes called 'Integrated Pollution Control' (IPC). This will be introduced in stages over the period from 1 April 1991 to 1 November 1995. A series of guidance notes is being issued by HMIP for all the main industrial processes and these will provide the basis for applications and subsequent determination. The smaller industrial installations are licensed by the environmental health departments of local authorities but in these cases only the emissions to the atmosphere are considered. HMIP will determine the larger applications and will take into account the total emissions including those to air, land and water, with reference to the principles of Best Practicable Environmental Option (BPEO) and Best Available Techniques Not Entailing Excessive Costs (BATNEEC).

The applications, representations from statutory consultees (but not from the general public or public interest groups), the licences and monitoring results may be viewed at the local authority in whose area the process operates.

For the larger and more polluting processes copies of the application can be seen either at the offices of the local authority, the NRA or HMIP.

D) Information that is not held on these public registers or is not published
This is more difficult to obtain but can also be the most useful information because it may be specific to an individual or group's particular interest.

Although there are about 150 British Acts that *prohibit* the provision of information to the public there are three important pieces of recent legislation that should have improved access to environmental information. These are:
  i) Statutory Instrument 1988 No.1199 The Town and Country Planning (Assessment of Environmental Effects) Regulations 1988 — this is the incorporation of an EC directive (85/337/EEC) into British Law
  ii) The Local Government (Access to Information) Act 1985
  iii) The Environmental Information Regulations 1992
(Other legislation such as The Environmental Protection Act 1990

and the Water Acts include sections to establish public registers but these are touched upon above.) I here examine each of the three in turn to see how they are relevant to information that may be needed:

i) Environmental Assessment

When major projects are proposed that may have a significant impact on the environment, the application must be supported by an Environmental Assessment. For certain types of project such as large power stations, radioactive waste stores and hazardous waste landfill sites, an Environmental Assessment is a mandatory requirement. For a wide range of less controversial projects, an environmental statement may be required if the development 'would be likely to have significant effects on the environment by virtue of its nature, size or location'. The public are allowed access to this document and must be able to purchase copies at 'a reasonable charge reflecting printing and distribution costs'. In practice this has meant that charges have ranged from none to £200.

The public and a range of statuary consultees including bodies such as the National Rivers Authority, the Countryside Council for Wales, the Health and Safety Executive etc. may comment upon the application, and their submissions, along with the environmental statement, become the 'Environmental Information' which must be considered by the relevant planning authority.

The problem of information technically being available, but at a price which makes it impractical, can be a serious one. When, for example, Nuclear Electric submitted a planning application for an incinerator to burn off contaminated oil at Trawsfynydd they provided a slim environmental statement in support of the proposal. A local organisation, *Cadno*, used a consultant to assess the application and its implications but to do this the consultant needed information about the doses to critical groups, which should have been part of the application. Nuclear Electric said that there was no problem about providing the information but they would charge £4,500 — beyond the resources of the group.

The solution in cases where there is an excessive charge made for the provision of information is to ask an MP to take up the issue, and to raise it with Friends of the Earth or Greenpeace, as both groups acknowledge the fundamental importance of environmental information and are monitoring the implementation of European Community Directives relating to its provision. The more serious breaches may merit complaints to the Ombudsman (in the case of local authorities) or even a judicial review.

The EC directive on environmental assessment has been transposed into English and Welsh law so that environmental assessments are linked with planning applications. A consequence of this is that there are potential loopholes in those cases where no planning application is made, such as where permitted development rights might exist.

A recent example of this is the addition of a new rotary kiln incinerator on the Rechem site at Pontypool. Although this could prolong the lifetime of the controversial incineration operation for a further twenty years, no environmental application was required because the new incinerator was deemed to be permitted development by Torfaen Borough Council. Another area of concern is offshore drilling which is not covered by the normal planning system. It has been agreed that sites within twenty-five miles of the shore should produce an environmental assessment before commencing extraction, and to which the public may have access. Yet there is no obligation for any assessment if the well is further offshore or for exploratory drilling. This issue is the subject of a complaint to the European Commission by Friends of the Earth Cymru.

Major failings with many environmental statements are: a) the general lack of public consultation before they are prepared; b) a lack of objectivity. These often backfire on developers who find that the imposition of a scheme on a local population having no sense of 'ownership' or participation is extremely difficult — and can generate a hostile reaction. Ideally full public consultation should take place at the earliest stages. Environmental statements should not be documents that are drafted simply to support an application — they should objectively examine the implications of the proposed development on the environment from a neutral standpoint. Unfortunately, this rarely happens in practice.

ii) The Local Government (Access to Information) Act 1985
This legislation allows the public access to many of the meetings, agendas and reports in local administration. Particularly useful is

the section which gives the right to view 'background' papers. These are the information that has been considered by the officers in the preparation of their reports to members. Each report should have a list of the background papers attached, but this condition is often overlooked.

Unfortunately, local authorities may make a 'reasonable charge' simply for access to the files. Swansea City Council, for example, charge £13.45 per file plus any copying charges — a major deterrent to all but the most affluent information seeker. The challenges available in such cases are as noted above but with direct approach to local councillors being the most appropriate starting point.

iii) The Environmental Information Regulations 1992
These regulations implement another piece of European Community legislation — Council Directive 90/313/EEC — on the freedom of access to information on the environment. The objective of the EC directive is to: "...ensure freedom of access to and dissemination of, information on the environment held by public authorities and to set out the basic terms and conditions on which such information should be made available". It was on this second point that the UK implementation floundered and Friends of the Earth have already launched a complaint to the EU on the basis that the terms and conditions have not been defined but left to each body who may hold information to define the mechanisms of access for themselves.

The information covered by the regulations appears to be very broad — covering:
a) "the state of any water or air, the state of any flora or fauna, the state of any soil" or the state of any natural site or other land;
b) "any activities or measures (including activities giving rise to noise or any other nuisance) which adversely affect anything [mentioned in sub-paragraph (a) above] or are likely to adversely affect anything so mentioned;" and
c) "any activities or administrative or other measures (including any environmental management programmes) which are designed to protect anything so mentioned".

The regulations make it clear that this information should be made available to "every person who requests it". There is therefore no obligation to live locally or to declare an interest in the information before it is provided.

In spite of the apparent breadth of coverage there are a number of reasons that an authority *may* use to refuse disclosure including data held for the purposes of any judicial or legislative function, requests that are 'manifestly unreasonable' or formulated in too general a manner.

In practice many relevant authorities have not defined either the method of access or listed the information they hold. This could lead to the Catch 22 situation of having a request refused because it is 'too general', yet it being impossible to be specific because there is not enough detail about the information available.

Nonetheless the Environmental Information regulations should give the public much wider access to information about the environment. It is certainly worth quoting them to support any request for environmental data made to a local authority or government department.

A Few Statistics

Obtaining the information is only the first-stage. It is then necessary to interpret, calculate what you need and to present it.

"There are no facts" said Friedrich Nietzche, "only interpretations", and it is inevitable that any presentation of information will reflect the subjective choices of the author. In this section an attempt has been made to 'look beneath the surface' of the statistics that are available from official sources and to translate the information about, for example, traffic growth, into an analysis of the increased pollution that might be expected from that growth.

Wales is a relatively small country with a total area of 2,076,620 hectares and a resident population of 2,835,073 recorded on Census night of 21 April 1991. The population of Wales is reasonably stable having increased by only 21,400 since the 1981 Census — a growth rate of 0.08 per cent per year. This is very low compared with the greatest rate of change of population in Wales over the last century which was 0.22 per cent per year during the period from 1901-1911. The Welsh Office predicts that by the turn of the century the population will reach 2.98 million. The average population density is 1.4 persons per hectare which is low compared with the figure of 2.4 for Great Britain as a whole. The range within Wales is from 9.4 persons per hectare in South Glamorgan to only 0.2 persons per hectare in Powys.

Perhaps more significant in terms of the environmental impact of the Welsh population is the housing density. In 1991 there were 1,184,133 dwellings in the country of which 24.3 per cent were detached, 30.1 per cent semi-detached and 33.1 per cent terraced housing. Average household size is currently about 2.61 people but by the year 2000 the number of households is expected to increase by 60,000 to 1.16 million and average household size to fall to 2.52. Clearly this will intensify the pressure upon the environment for new housing land.

Spending on the Environment

Welsh Office figures show that Wales is the recipient of £9,343 million of the central government expenditure that can be geographically attributed. This amounts to £3,268 per person which is about seven per cent above the UK average. Spending on programmes within the responsibility of the Secretary of State for Wales is £5,307 million which equates to £1,721 per head. For the financial year 1991-2 The Welsh Office spent 3.5 per cent of this money (£186.9 million) on 'Environmental Services' which included £32.5 million on the Cardiff Bay Development Corporation (projected to increase to £45 million in 1993-4) and £36.1 million on the Main Urban Programme to "stimulate enterprise and the creation of jobs". The Countryside Council for Wales received £14.5 million for the year and the National Parks grant was £3.8 million which is equivalent to less than 0.4 pence per person per day for the Welsh population.

The average expenditure on environmental health in Wales by local authorities amounts to 2.2 pence per person per day which has to cover everything from catching stray dogs to inspecting and monitoring tips receiving 'special' waste. By way of comparison this is about one third of the average amount we pay as a subsidy to nuclear power as a hidden premium on our electricity bills. The expenditure on roads, meanwhile, for 1992-3 was about 46 pence per person per day.

Nature Conservation

There is a great deal to commend the environment of Wales and this is reflected in the popularity of the country with tourists. Tourism has become a major source of both income and employment and shows the importance of an attractive environment to creating jobs. Total expenditure by tourists is about £1.26 billion and generates approximately 80,000 full-time-equivalent jobs making up more than nine per cent of employment in Wales.

The areas that are particularly attractive to visitors are the wild countryside and the surf-swept beaches. The protection given to these facilities appears to be impressive.

Snowdonia has been a National Park since 1951 and by 1957, with the designation of the Brecon Beacons and the Pembrokeshire Coast, Wales benefited from 409,800 hectares of National Park. This is 19.7 per cent of the total area of Wales.

Gower was the first Area of Outstanding Natural Beauty (AONB) in Great Britain when it was designated in 1957. Another four AONBs have since brought the total area up to 83,000 hectares or about four per cent of the country.

Areas with Statutory Protection:

	Number	Area in Hectares
National Nature Reserve	49	13,359
Local Nature Reserve	19	3,423
Sites of Special Scientific Interest	870	205,653
Special Protection Area	8	23,797
Ramsar Sites	6	23,582
Marine Nature Reserve	1	1,500

(As at 31 March 1993. Source: Countryside Council for Wales)

In all, over thirty-three per cent of the area of Wales had some form of statutory landscape conservation definition by 1991, and this is likely to increase significantly when the full agreements are reached on environmentally sensitive areas. A further total of over 20,000 hectares was protected by organisations like the wildlife trusts and the Royal Society for the Protection of Birds. The coast-line of Wales has also been well designated — by 1992 over 495 kilometres was defined as Heritage Coast — which is forty-two per cent of the total coast.

Unfortunately most of the designations do not give the level of protection that is needed. In some cases this is because the threats are outside the control of the Countryside Council for Wales. Examples include radiation from the accident at Chernobyl, to alleviate the effects of which the Welsh Office has had to spend between £0.6 and £0.7 million every year. Other threats are outside the protection given by the designations such as operations already authorised by planning permission.

Amongst the major direct threats to the environment of Wales are:

Mineral Extraction and Opencast

Aggregates

Wales has good reserves of a wide range of minerals. There are currently more than fifty limestone quarries in operation, approximately fifteen sandstone quarries and about fifteen sites extracting igneous rock. Sand and gravel are dredged from offshore banks in South Wales and dug from land in the north. The output from these quarries rose by forty-four per cent in the four years from 1985 and demand is increasing rapidly. For England and Wales the demand in 1948 was 57 million tonnes and this had risen to about 300 million tonnes by 1989. There was a fifty per cent increase in the demand for construction aggregates in the 1980s alone.

Since 1989, demand has dropped but it is estimated that demand for England and Wales will rise to between 370 and 440 million tonnes by 2011. Central government demand forecasts show that, over the twenty years to 2011, North Wales will need to produce 260 million tonnes of primary aggregates of which fifty-four per cent would be for export, mainly to the north-west of England; and production in the south would need to be 280 million tonnes of which twenty-nine per cent would be for export to England. The proportion of aggregate required for export is expected to increase over the period to 2011, by when, up to about eighty per cent for North Wales and to about fifty-five per cent for South Wales minerals are likely to be exported. To meet the projected demand the levels of extraction would have to increase by forty per cent over the peak production of 1989.

Threats to valuable countryside are already being made for mineral extraction and the procedure of registering a type of old planning permission — interim development orders (IDOs) — has led to a widespread conflict with areas of nature conservation.

In 1993, a study by Friends of the Earth Cymru showed that there were a total of similar eighty-eight IDO applications covering a total area of over 5,000 acres. Of these seventy-one have already been registered and only ten were rejected or 'not determined'. (Nearly half of the rejections were in Mid Glamorgan.)

Amongst the conflicts highlighted were the following applications for registration:

13 with Areas of Outstanding Natural Beauty (AONBs) covering 879.32 acres;

17 Sites of Special Scientific Interest (SSSI) conflicts covering 2,277.34 acres;

1 on an Ancient Monument covering 101.27 acres;

7 with Heritage Coastlines covering 550.81 acres;

12 in National Parks covering 1,054.69 acres.

Under the terms of the legislation an application for registration could not be refused because it was in conflict with a nature conservation area. As a consequence, many of our most important wildlife sites have no protection from old mineral permissions.

Opencast Mining

Opencasting is a particularly damaging land use which was described by the House of Commons Select Energy Committee as "one of the most environmentally destructive processes being carried out in the UK".

There are effectively two exposed coalfields within Wales. In the north the geology is more disparate and the coalfield consists of two main areas in Clwyd with a small field in Anglesey. It is in South Wales that the largest and most attractive field for opencasting lie. It covers 2,000 sq. km and stretches from Gwent to Dyfed with the broadest part being in the west of Mid Glamorgan. The demise of deep mining has left opencast coal as the main method of extraction of coal in Wales. The total UK production for opencast coal in 1991-2 was 16.7 million tonnes from 57 sites. The Welsh contribution to this total was 2 million tonnes. The sites in Wales cover up to 2,500 hectares each year, of which about fourteen per cent could be considered as derelict land clearance. The vast majority of opencast mining takes place on greenfield sites. A recent opencast planning permission at Selar grasslands in the Neath Valley will completely destroy an SSSI which is home to the rare Marsh Fritillary butterfly.

Oil and Gas Exploration
A relatively new and recent threat to the Welsh environment is offshore drilling for oil and gas. The Department of Trade and Industry issues licences for exploration and drilling for 'blocks' of the seabed. In 1993 the results of the fourteenth round of licence applications were announced and more than twenty licences have been issued for blocks close to the Welsh coast. The majority of these are close to St. David's Head but large areas have been licensed in Cardigan Bay and adjacent to the shore on the North Wales coast, around the Great Orme. The sixteenth round 'consultation, was carried out in 1994 in spite of increasing evidence of damage to cetaceans and one of Britain's very few colonies of bottle-nosed dolphins in Cardigan Bay.

Industrial Pollution

Industrial pollution may be found on the site of the industry; in areas around the site from wind-blown dust and deposition of pollutants from chimneys; in streams, rivers or the sea into which discharges are made; in sewage sludge if waste is disposed of to sewers; around landfill or incinerator sites used to dispose of waste products; or much further afield via the long range transport of pollutants in the atmosphere.

Acid Rain
Wales is highly vulnerable to damage by acid rain. A study of 51

Sites of Special Scientific Interest in Mid and North Wales under-taken by the Countryside Council for Wales indicated that:

29 per cent were (a) "almost certainly acidified"

22 per cent were (b) "at least occasionally acidified"

31 per cent probably belonged to either (a) or (b)

and only 18 per cent were classed as "probably not at risk"

In some areas of North Wales over seventy-five per cent of the land will still exceed its critical load by 2005 even assuming the United Kingdom meets targets set for acid gas reductions.

The omens for this are not promising. The 1993 National Plan Allocation and HMIP limits allow Aberthaw A & B power stations to emit 90,000 tonnes of sulphur dioxide and 36,000 tonnes of oxide of nitrogen. In spite of hopes of reductions in acid gas emissions from power stations in England and Wales under Integrated Pollution Control, and the clear need for this, the emission limits placed by HMIP have been disappointing. The Environmental Data Services journal *ENDS* reported that "the authorisations will probably not reduce the generators' overall emissions of acid gases by so much as an ounce".

Legacy from the Past — Contaminated Land

Wales has a long history of mining and industrial development. Unfortunately many of these activities were carried out with little regard for the pollution they caused. In many cases the land around the closed mines and factories is still highly contaminated by a range of toxic materials.

Contaminated land is not a new problem — the tailings (spoil heaps) from the lead mines of Roman Wales were perhaps the first serious contamination of this country. The subsequent decline of the Roman Empire, which has been attributed by some to the drinking of wine from lead goblets, may serve as a warning to those who would ignore the risks posed by heavy metals!

The numbers and locations of the sites of potentially contami-nated land are influenced by the physical geography of Wales. These were detailed by the Welsh Office report 'Contaminated Land in Wales' which was published in 1988. However, the report listed only the larger sites and did not include either those sites that had already been developed for housing or the majority of landfill sites in Wales.

There remains a real danger that the purchaser of a new property could be completely unaware that the site was previously used, for example, as a gas works and be heavily contaminated with acid tars and phenols. The Government has been attempting to address the issue but, in March 1993 after intensive lobbying and pressure from the construction industry they backed down from implementing legislation that would have required local authorities to prepare public registers of contaminated land.

Without such public registers, finding information about contamination can be difficult. Although contamination should be a consideration for building regulations, many authorities in Wales hold very little data. However, it is worth trying both the planning and the environmental health departments of the district council before resorting to the time consuming searches of old maps that are the standard method of identifying potentially contaminating uses. A survey by Friends of the Earth Cymru in 1992, highlights 968 potentially contaminated sites covering a total area of over 4,500 hectares. These were only the largest sites and the survey excluded those where development had taken place. There may be between ten and fifteen thousand contaminated sites around Wales in total.

Waste Disposal
About 10.3 million tonnes of waste are produced in Wales every year. This includes about 1,500,000 tonnes of domestic and commercial waste and 2.4 million tonnes of industrial waste of which 89,193 tonnes were special waste in 1990-91. Special waste is defined as that which would be likely to kill or seriously injure a child weighing 20 kg if they ingested not more than 5 cc of the material. In theory, special waste production in Wales has the potential to kill or seriously injure about 17 billion children.

The majority of the domestic waste disposed of in Wales is buried in landfill sites of which there are currently over 200 licensed to accept waste. The average net cost of refuse disposal for 1991-2 was £8 per tonne but some areas paid much less than this — Wrexham and Cynon Valley for example, paid £4 per tonne and Port Talbot only £3. The low cost of landfill disposal reflects the low level of engineering work (gas control, leachate treatment etc.) associated with the typical landfill sites in Wales. Figures from the Royal Commission on Environmental Pollution estimate that the cost of providing a 50,000 tonne per annum landfill site is £14.38 per tonne.

Collection costs are higher than disposal charges with the Welsh average being £21 per tonne; Delyn manages to do the job for £13 per tonne. Even the domestic waste, although simply classified as 'controlled' rather than as 'special' still contains a wide range of contamination. It is likely that the total domestic waste production of Wales will contain the following contaminants:

| | Range in grams per tonne | | Mass landfilled/Incinerated (kg) | |
	Max	Min	Max	Min
Iron	75,000	23,000	112,500,000	34,500,000
Zinc	3,500	1,300	5,250,000	1,950,000
Lead	2,500	800	3,750,000	1,200,000
Cadmium	40	6	60,000	9,000
Mercury	7	2	10,500	3,000
Copper	2,500	420	3,750,000	630,000
Chromium	450	100	675,000	150,000
Nickel	200	60	300,000	90,000

(Calculated from 'Review of Municipal Solid Waste Incineration in the UK' Warren Springs Laboratory.)

The landfill sites into which the waste is deposited will eventually leak, even if they are lined with modern plastics. The heavy metals in the waste could then pollute either the groundwater under the landfill or the surface water around it. For landfill locations such as the site at Pen-y-Bont on the River Dee such leakage could be disastrous — more than 2.2 million people in North Wales and Merseyside draw their water downstream of a tip that has been given planning permission in an oxbow bend of the river.

Control of Industrial Major Accident Hazards (CIMAH)
The majority of industrial emissions to the environment are the results of discharges from processes operating on a day to day basis. Occasionally however there is a catastrophic release as a

result of an industrial accident. Chernobyl was one example; the Flixborough explosion in 1973 and Seveso disaster in 1976 (where dioxin was spread over land around a chemical plant after an explosion) and Bhopal in 1984 were others. After Seveso, the European Community laid down regulations that required a special system of licensing for industrial sites with the potential for major accidents. The Health and Safety Executive now list 26 such sites in Wales, mainly oil and gas storage depots.

Sea and Water Pollution

Wales has 1,179 km of coastline along which there are fifty-one designated bathing beaches and nearly 140 outfalls pumping raw or minimally treated sewage. A higher percentage of the population of Dŵr Cymru customers than any other water service company are connected to sea outfalls, but in 1992 only about twenty-seven per cent of sewage outfalls serving forty-five per cent of the population receive secondary treatment (i.e. anything more than settlement or filtration). This is reflected in the failure of eleven of the designated beaches to meet the minimum standards set by the European Community in 1992.

Dŵr Cymru claim that by 1998 they will be able to 'virtually guarantee' that none of their sewage treatment works will be responsible for a failure at any of Wales' 'top bathing beaches'. This is the standard that should have been met by 1985 under the European Community Bathing Water Directive.

By 1998 the dumping of sewage at sea must also stop. Dŵr Cymru have already stopped sea disposal, whilst North West Water are likely to continue sea disposal in Liverpool Bay, where they annually dispose of over 1.8 million tonnes, until the licences for sea disposal are terminated.

Industrial effluents are collected together with domestic discharges to sewers, thus sewage sludge is generally contaminated with heavy metals. The total discharges of heavy metals in Liverpool Bay due to sewage sludge is estimated below:

Tonnes per annum	Cadmium	Chromium	Mercury	Copper	Nickel	Lead	Zinc
	0.35	13.6	0.176	22.6	3.6	21.8	47.6

Transport

There are few communities of any size that remain unaffected by the spiralling increase in car ownership and use.

The number of vehicles licensed in Wales has increased by thirty per cent since 1980 and although there was a small drop in 1991, the trend is firmly upwards.

Vehicles Licensed in Wales

1980	934,671
1985	1,038,876
1987	1,094,179
1988	1,188,564
1990	1,222,018
1991	1,208,572

The Welsh Office figures forecast that the increase in road traffic in Wales will be slightly lower than in Great Britain with an increase of between thirty-nine per cent and sixty-six per cent by 2010. If these predictions prove to be accurate and were to be equally distributed across the country then the total distance travelled on major roads by 2010 in each county are illustrated in the figure below:

Volume of Major Road Traffic by County (Billion Vehicle/Km)

		1986	1990	1995	2000	2005	2010
Clwyd	Low	2.16	2.14	2.35	2.55	2.76	2.97
	High			2.50	2.87	3.21	3.55
Dyfed	Low	1.64	1.61	1.77	1.92	2.08	2.24
	High			1.88	2.16	2.42	2.67
Gwent	Low	2.02	2.05	2.26	2.44	2.64	2.85
	High						
Gwynedd	Low	1.49	1.45	1.60	1.73	1.87	2.02
	High			1.70	1.94	2.18	2.41
Mid Glam	Low	2.08	2.07	2.28	2.46	2.67	2.88
	High			2.42	2.77	3.11	3.44
Powys	Low	0.74	0.74	0.81	0.88	0.95	1.03
	High			0.87	0.99	1.11	1.23
S. Glam	Low	1.06	1.11	1.22	1.32	1.43	1.54
	High			1.30	1.49	1.67	1.84

W. Glam	Low	1.34	1.38	1.52	1.64	1.78	1.92
	High			1.61	1.85	2.07	2.29
Wales	Low	12.53	12.55	13.81	14.93	16.19	17.4
	High			14.68	16.82	18.83	20.8

1986 and 1990 figures are for actual distances.

Not only will the new traffic greatly increase the burdens upon the road network but it will also generate much more pollution. The extra carbon dioxide produced by the increased car traffic alone would amount to over 1.3 million tonnes. To calculate the approximate emissions to air from cars (in grams) multiply the number of cars by the distance travelled in km by the following factors:

	g/km
Carbon Monoxide	6.40
Hydrocarbons	0.93
Lead	0.02
NO_x	1.00
CO_2	190.00

Access — Some Comparisons

A booklet titled 'What you don't know *will* hurt you — Environmental Information as a basic human right' was launched in 1992. Another offering from Greenpeace or Friends of the Earth you might think — but you would be wrong. In fact the publication was produced (on unchlorinated paper) by the Nordic Council of Ministers and distributed through the ministers of the environment in Sweden, Denmark, Norway, Finland and Iceland.

The document was full of talk about links between access to information and democracy, participation in decision making by all affected by the decisions, of international responsibility and of governments working closely with non-governmental organisations. This may not seem very relevant to the environment of Wales but the report highlights a very significant difference in attitude between Britain and the Nordic nations in relation to access to information and the protection of the environment. When the Environmental Information regulations were brought into force in England and Wales on 31 December 1992, the Welsh

Office did not even issue a press release to inform the public of their new rights to information and no bilingual information about the legislation was available until the end of the summer.

The concept of wider access to information, even about the environment, has been difficult for UK authorities, hardened by years of secrecy, to accept. We still have only limited access to much information even if we are directly affected by the matter in question. Yet such access has been available to the Danes since 1886, and in 1970 all persons were granted a common right of access, with few exceptions, to information on the public administration. The right even applies to people who are not Danish and do not live in Denmark.

Nor is it only the progressive Scandinavian countries that are ahead of the UK in the provision of information. The United States allows citizens to link to their registers by modem, and even provides data via the Internet. They also produce a computer-readable compact disk which allows anyone with the appropriate drive on their computer to analyse details of all the toxic releases from industrial processes across the whole country. As a trial the author sent requests for information to Her Majesty's Inspectorate of Pollution and to the United States Environmental Protection Agency (USEPA) on the same day. The USEPA replied and sent comprehensive data before HMIP had even acknowledged the request. HMIP took a further two months to provide the information required.

Forces for Change — European Commission Legislation

Environmental legislation in Wales generally matches that of England with only minor difference in the mechanism of control — waste regulation authorities in Wales, for example, are district councils rather than the county councils that have the responsibility in England. Another example is that recycling is supported in England by a series of supplementary credit approvals to local authorities whereas in Wales money is distributed as a lump sum and the priorities and distribution to different budgets is a matter for each local authority. A disturbing trend is emerging, however, in that some of the more progressive planning guidance is being implemented in England while adoption in Wales is being delayed.

Although statutes are published by parliament, the real driving force behind UK environmental legislation is the European Union. Increasing numbers of laws and regulations are being issued by Brussels — there have been nearly 400 items of EC (or EU as it is now) environmental legislation since 1967 when the first measure was adopted. Recently there has been something of a backlash against the costs of meeting the increasing demands of the EU in Britain. This is reflected in comments emphasising the importance of subsidiarity in environmental legislation made by the (then) Environment Minister David Maclean in a speech to the Financial Times Water Conference (16 March 1993 —DoE Press Release no 171). Mr Maclean suggested that the bathing water and drinking water directives were out of date and that standards for parameters such as pesticides, nitrites and polyaromatic hydrocarbons had been wrongly set and should be adjusted. Such adjustment would, he inferred, be less demanding than current standards.

The Government has established a Deregulation Unit and it is no secret that environmental legislation is targeted to reduce the constraints that some industrialists claim this legislation is placing on growth. Increasingly vulnerable is the European Community legislation and some of the requirements for industry to make information about their monitoring available to the public (indeed the latest trends are to dispense with emissions monitoring altogether and rely on analysis of filter dust). Such 'monitoring' is of little or no use for giving warnings about process upsets and the corrections that may be needed, because the data will be inevitably well out of date. There may also be an added incentive to fit less effective filters in order to avoid catching too much pollution. Such trends need to be carefully watched.

On the other hand conservationists are still optimistic about the potential for EU legislation to deliver protection that is sadly lacking in UK legislation. The impending complete loss of the Site of Special Scientific Interest at Selar Grasslands, for example, may prove to be a test case for the effectiveness of the EU Habitats directive.

Wales is a spectacular country with a sensitive environment and by using environmental information effectively each of us can help to protect and improve our environment. We will also help to ensure the flow of data is not reduced. It is vital that we adopt the slogan of the American Chemical Industries Association: 'don't just trust polluters — track them!'.

Notes on Contributors

John Barnie is the editor of *Planet* magazine. His most recent publications include a study of the blues in Welsh, *Y Felan a Finnau* (University of Wales Press), and two collections of poems and fiction, *The Confirmation* and *The City* (Gomer).

Neil Caldwell was recently appointed Director of the Prince of Wales Committee after nearly seven years as Director of the Campaign for the Protection of Rural Wales. He has a doctorate in the Earth Sciences, is a past president of NUS Wales, and has worked for the National Trust in North and South Wales. He is a member of the NRA's Welsh Advisory Committee, Vice Chair of Wales Wildlife and Countryside Link, a Fellow of the Royal Society for the Arts and a member of the Welsh Language Board.

Rory Francis became Administrator of the Snowdonia National Park Society in 1994. For the four years previous to this he worked as Projects and Local Groups Officer with Friends of the Earth Cymru. A frequent contributor to radio and television programmes within Wales, in Welsh and Engliah, he is keen to help urge politicians and public towards a sustainable development agenda.

Alwyn Jones is a Principal Lecturer in Sociology at the University of Glamorgan and recently led the development of the inter-disciplinary B.A. (Hons) Environment and Social Values degree which received its first intake of students in 1993. His publications include *Rural Housing: The Agricultural Tied Cottage* (1975) and articles in *The Ecologist* and *The Sociological Review*.

Nic Lampkin is an agricultural economist working in the Department of Agricultural Sciences at the University of Wales in

Aberystwyth. His research interests include organic farming systems and agri-environmental policy. He is the author of a recent book entitled *Organic Farming*, and joint editor of the forthcoming *Economics of Organic Farming: an International Perspective*.

Peter Midmore is an agricultural economist working in the department of Agricultural Sciences at the University of Wales, Aberystwyth. His research interests are in the field of rural development, especially with regard to its interaction with the natural and cultural environment. His most recent publication is *Input-Output Models and the Agricultural Sector*, an edited collection of papers dealing with specific modelling approaches.

Margaret Minhinnick is a teacher and founder of the environmental pressure group Friends of the Earth Cymru, of which she was Co-ordinator between 1984 and 1994. She is currently engaged in establishing *Sustainable Wales*, which will be dedicated to profiling the best environmental practices and ideas, especially where they might influence employment, education and health.

Robert Minhinnick, the editor of this book, is a writer who has published six volumes of poetry and a book of essays entitled *Watching the Fire Eater*, which was Welsh Book of the Year in 1993. His *A Postcard Home: Tourism in the Mid Nineties* appeared this year in the 'Changing Wales' series from Gomer.

Alan Watson is a writer and researcher who lives on the Gower and works for Friends of the Earth Cymru. His articles on subjects such as the legacy of contaminated land, water pollution and waste incineration have appeared in *The Ecologist*, *New Scientist* and *Planet*.

Dr Phil Williams is a Professor of Physics at the University of Wales, Aberystwyth. He is at present involved in building an advanced radar on Svalbard to study the atmosphere and ionosphere over the Polar Cap. An active member of Plaid Cymru for over thirty years he has served several times as National Chairman and as Vice-President. At present he is the party spokesperson on Energy and the Environment.